GCSE

MATHS INVESTIGATIONS

TEACHERS' GUIDE

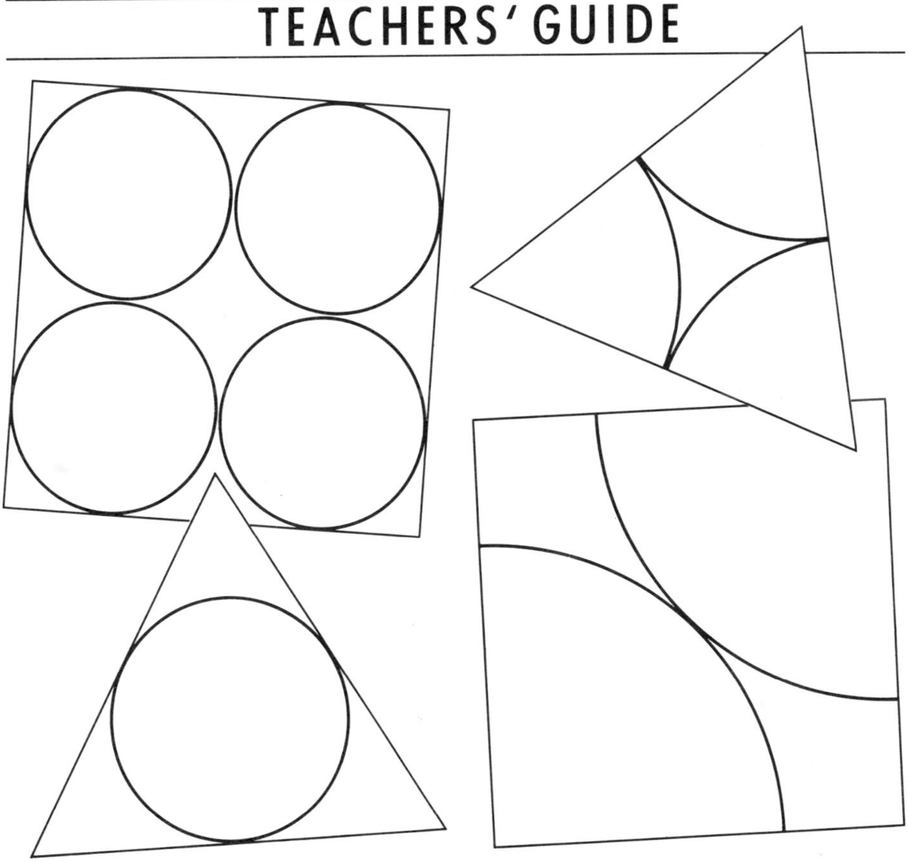

DAVID KIRKBY and PETER PATILLA

Hutchinson Education

Hutchinson Education

An imprint of Century Hutchinson Ltd
62 – 65 Chandos Place, London WC2N 4NW

Century Hutchinson Australia Pty Ltd
PO Box 496, 16 – 22 Church Street, Hawthorn,
Victoria 3122, Australia

Century Hutchinson New Zealand Ltd
PO Box 40-086, Glenfield, Auckland 10, New Zealand

Century Hutchinson South Africa (Pty) Ltd
PO Box 337, Bergvlei, 2012 South Africa

First published 1987

Typeset in 12pt Metrolight by
The Pen and Ink Book Company Ltd, London

Printed and bound in Great Britain

Produced by AMR for Hutchinson Education

Kirkby, David
GCSE Maths Investigations.
Teacher's guide.
1. Mathematics–1961-
I. Title II. Patilla, Peter
510 QA39.2

ISBN-0-09-173233-6

CONTENTS

The Cards

GCSE Maths Investigations contains 80 cards based on ten themes:

1 Area	**6 Powers**
2 Chains	**7 Rectangles**
3 Hexagons	**8 Paths**
4 Cards	**9 Number**
5 Triangles	**10 Shape**

There are eight cards for each theme.

The theme title provides an indication of a common identity for the eight cards in the set. Although, for example, a set of cards has the theme title 'Triangles', investigations involving triangles will arise from cards with other theme titles. There is no order to the eight cards within each theme.

Using the cards

GCSE Maths Investigations will complement any school's mathematics scheme and is very flexible.

△ It fits naturally into any individualised scheme.
△ It can act as a resource bank to suit the needs of a small group of children at any particular time.
△ It can be used in investigations where:

all pupils are involved in the same investigation

pupils are involved in a variety of investigations based on the same theme

pupils are involved in investigations of their own choice.

In whatever way the cards are used it must be stressed that they merely provide a *starting point* for some mathematical study. Each activity can be developed in many different directions involving mathematics at various levels.

The cards are not a set that need to be 'worked through'. It is possible that several lessons' work may arise from any particular card. It is hoped that pupils will become sufficiently interested in an investigation to continue in depth. It is better for a pupil to have completed one or two investigations in depth rather than to have tried several superficially.

It is intended that pupils will learn to develop their own lines of enquiry. The ability to do this does not come naturally to most pupils and therefore needs to be developed by the teacher through discussion and suggestions. The teachers' notes provide some possibilites for points of discussion, questions and extensions.

Although the teachers' notes suggest some *possible* solutions, they are not *answers*. It is important that pupils are not manoeuvred towards particular solutions. The value of investigational work is to enable pupils to develop thought processes and strategies for themselves.

Supplementing the cards

The cards provide a resource bank of starting points, which can be easily supplemented by the addition of teacher-made cards. Sources of ideas for these include:

The Investigator
SMILE CENTRE, Middle School Row, Kensal Raod, London

Investigation Bank Books
D. Kirkby: Eigen Publications, 39, Den Bank Crescent, Sheffield, S10 5PB

Peak Plus (Books 3 and 4) and *Investigation Posters*
A. Brighouse, D. Godber, P. Patilla: Thomas Nelson and Sons Ltd

Mathematical Activities and *More Mathematical Activities*
Brian Boult: Cambridge University Press

Sources of Mathematical Discovery and *Investigations in Mathematics*
Lorraine Mottershead: Basil Blackwell

Thinking Things Through
Leone Burton: Basil Blackwell

Mathematics Teaching and other publications
ATM: Kings Chambers, Queen Street, Derby

Mathematics in School
Mathematics Association: 259, London Road, Leicester

Pupils Work

An important aspect of investigation work is the opportunity provided for pupils to communicate their mathematics: by 'write-ups' describing how they went about the investigation and by short periods of class discussion where ideas can be pooled. It is important that pupils develop the ability to write and explain their thinking clearly.

It is a good idea for each pupil to have a loose leaf 'Investigations Log Book' which has a pocket for the various pieces of simple apparatus which accompany some of the investigations and which allow the inclusion of different forms of stationery as well as allowing the pupil to add to investigations previously attempted. These log books can be simply made by the pupils themselves:

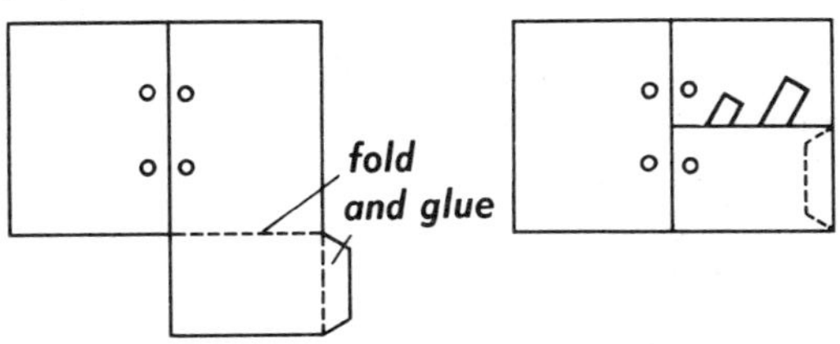

It is important that pupils have the opportunity of returning to an investigation.

Creative stimulus can arise from 'Investigation Corners' in which a starting point is given and the resulting work displayed.

Materials

The cards are activity based and require the pupils to use simple and inexpensive materials as an integral part of the investigation. The importance of allowing pupils the opportunity of handling the materials cannot be over emphasised.

Materials and stationery should be easily accessible to pupils.

Apparatus required

Geoboards	Squares (about 2 cm) card or plastic
Counters	Calculators
Compasses	Cubes
Gummed reinforcements	Matchsticks
Card	Number cards
Tracing paper	Scissors
	Plain paper
	Glue (glue-sticks are ideal)
	Special papers (see Copy masters)

Number Cards: These are small pieces of card (approx. 5 x 8 cm) on which numbers are written, usually in the 0–25 range.

Copy master

There are ten A4 Copy master sheets to accompany the cards:

1 1 cm isometric
2 2 cm isometric
3 1 cm square
4 2 cm square
5 Table of primes
6 1 cm square dot
7 1 cm isometric dot
8 Table of squares
9 Hexagon paper
10 Number cards

These sheets are free from copyright and may be duplicated in whatever form the teacher wishes.

Suppliers

Squares; Geoboards; Counters; Cubes – these are available from:

Tarquin Publications, Stradbroke, Diss, Norfolk
E.J. Arnold, Parkside Lane, Dewsbury Road, Leeds

Number Cards are available from:
Eigen Publications, 39, Den Bank Crescent, Sheffield S10 5PB

AREA

	APPARATUS	ACTIVITY
1 Squares	Dotty paper	Drawing squares with different areas
2 Surrounds	Squares 2cm squared paper	Areas of surrounding shapes
3 Equal shares	Squared paper	Dividing squares into two equal areas
4 In and out	Squared paper	Areas and perimeters of shapes
5 Cubists	Cubes	Surface area of models built from cubes
6 Portions	Compasses	Areas of parts of circles
7 Reinforcements	Gummed reinforcements	Areas involving parts of circles
8 Challenge	Dotty paper	Area of polygons

These cards contain a variety of experiences associated with **area** ranging from areas of squares, rectangles and other polygons to areas of circles and parts of circles. Other activities involve pupils in exploring surface area and also in investigations based on relationships between area and perimeter.

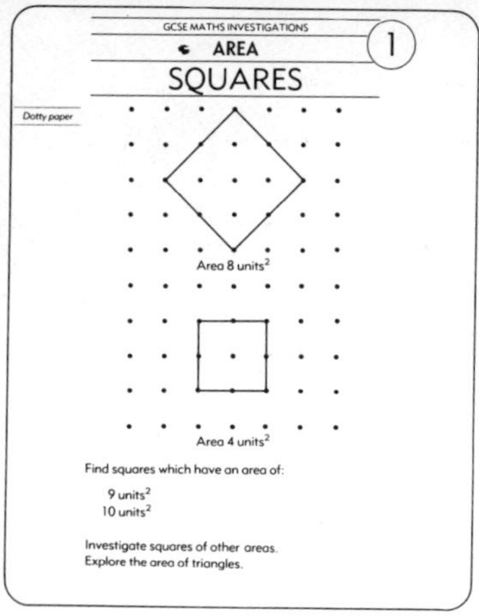
GCSE MATHS INVESTIGATIONS
AREA
SQUARES
1
Dotty paper

Area 8 units^2

Area 4 units^2

Find squares which have an area of:

9 units^2
10 units^2

Investigate squares of other areas.
Explore the area of triangles.

GCSE MATHS INVESTIGATIONS

AREA

SQUARES

1

Square dotty paper

△ Some possible areas:

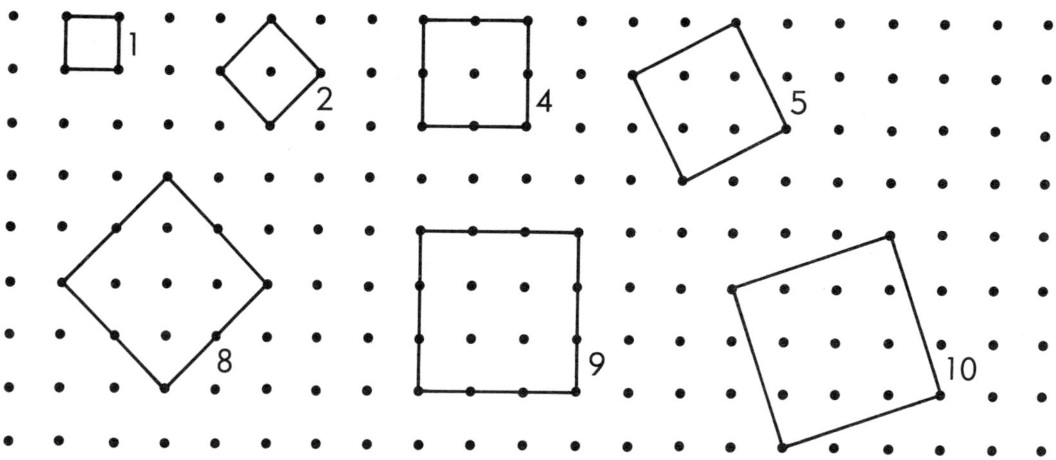

△ For an area of 5, the square must have a side of $\sqrt{(1^2 + 2^2)}$

For an area of 8, the square must have a side of $\sqrt{(2^2 + 2^2)}$

For an area of 10, the square must have a side of $\sqrt{(3^2 + 1^2)}$

△ Consider the sums of two square numbers:

+	1	4	9	16	25 →
1	2	5	10	17	26
4		8	13	20	29
9			18	25	34
16				32	41
25					50
↓					

Possible areas of squares are:
1, 2, 4, 5, 8, 9, 10, 13, 16, 17, 18, 20...

△ Investigate the area of triangles.
Use isometric dotty paper to investigate triangles, parallelograms and regular hexagons.

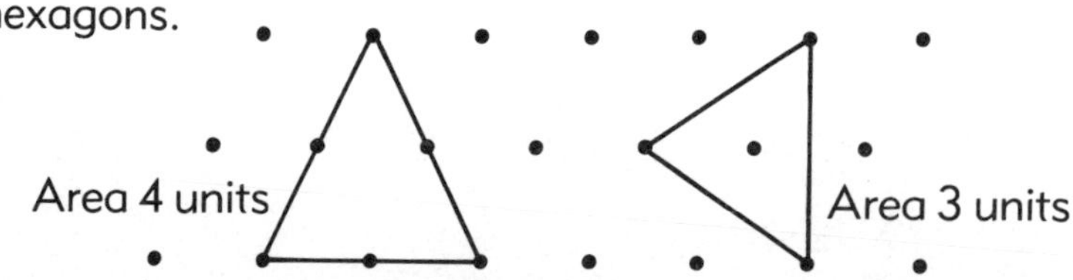

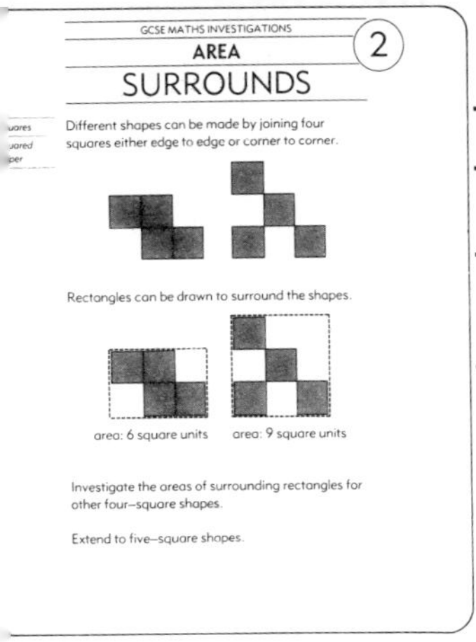
GCSE MATHS INVESTIGATIONS

AREA

SURROUNDS

2

Different shapes can be made by joining four squares either edge to edge or corner to corner.

Rectangles can be drawn to surround the shapes.

area: 6 square units   area: 9 square units

Investigate the areas of surrounding rectangles for other four-square shapes.

Extend to five-square shapes.

GCSE MATHS INVESTIGATIONS

AREA

SURROUNDS

2

Squares

Squared paper

△ Four-square shapes:

edge to edge

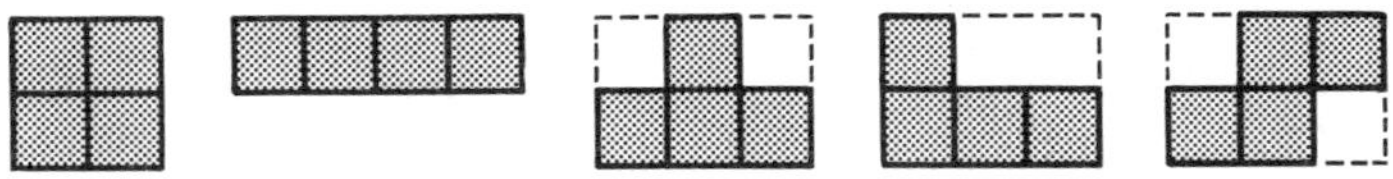

surrounding area: 4 4 6 6 6

corner-to-corner

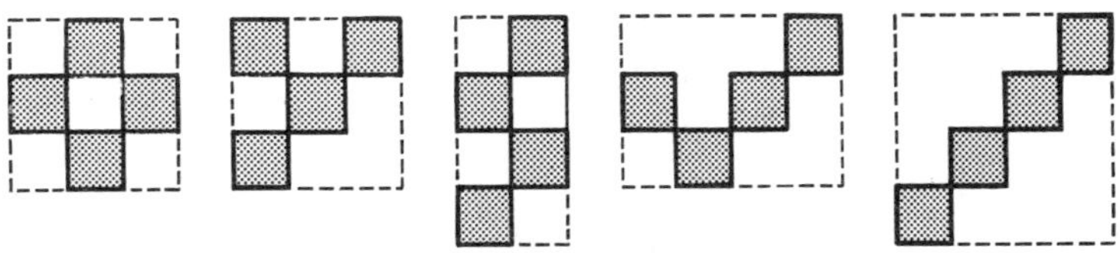

surrounding area: 9 9 8 12 16

△ Five-square shapes:
Examine those which are surrounded by squares:

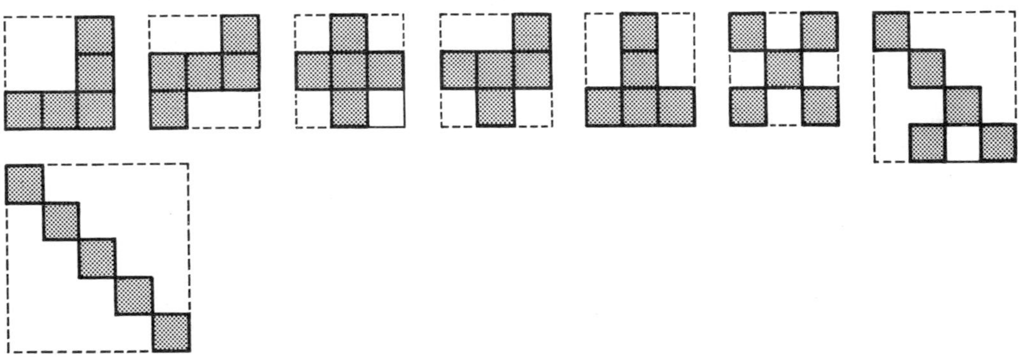

△ Investigate maximum and minimum surrounding areas for other numbers of squares when joined:

edge to edge corner to corner

△ How many different surrounding areas can be made with:

five squares? six squares....?

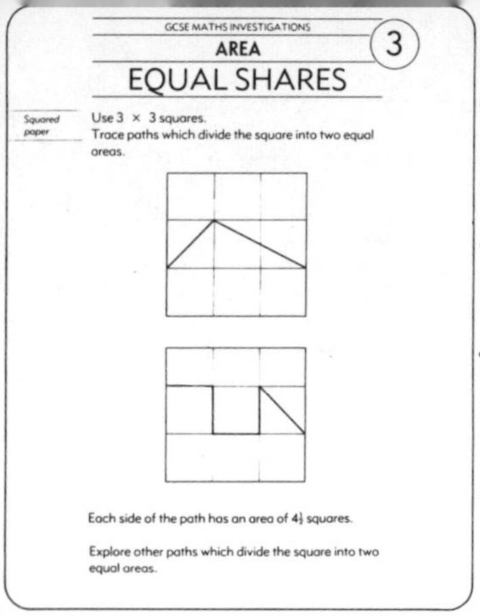
GCSE MATHS INVESTIGATIONS

AREA 3

EQUAL SHARES

Squared paper

Use 3 × 3 squares.
Trace paths which divide the square into two equal areas.

Each side of the path has an area of 4½ squares.

Explore other paths which divide the square into two equal areas.

GCSE MATHS INVESTIGATIONS

AREA

EQUAL SHARES

3

Squared paper

△ Consider the various ways of classifying the dissections:

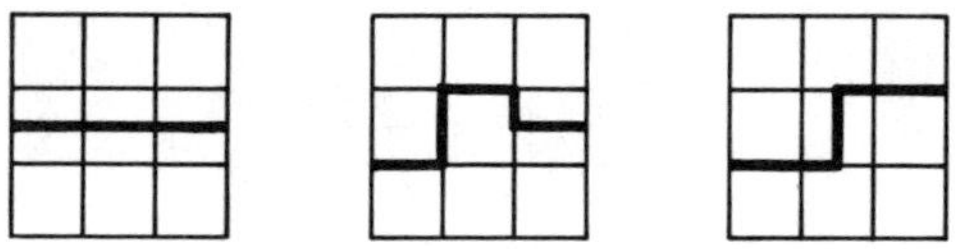
horizontal and vertical lines

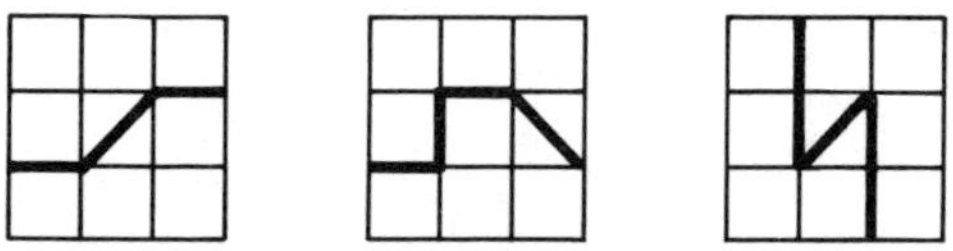
horizontal, vertical and diagonal lines

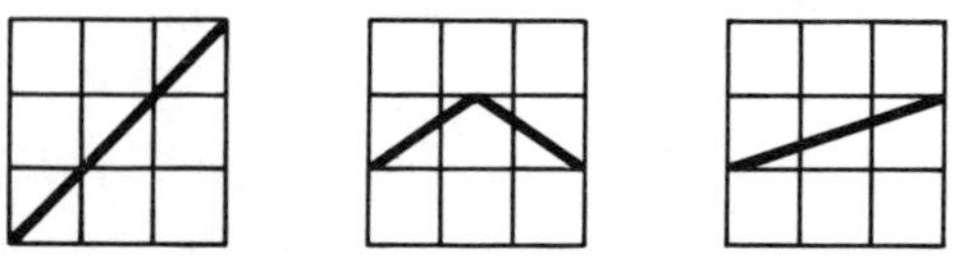
diagonal lines

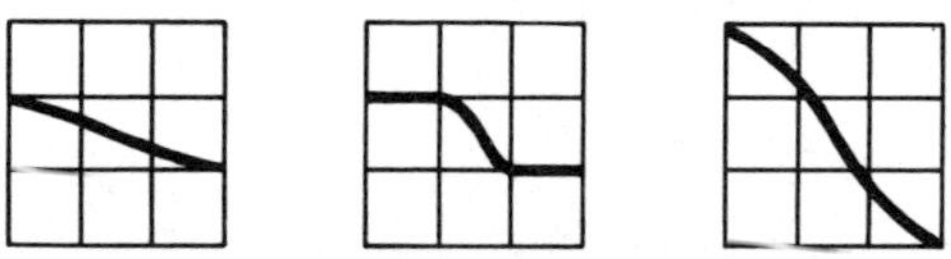
curved lines

△ Choose a vertex and find dissections which pass through it.

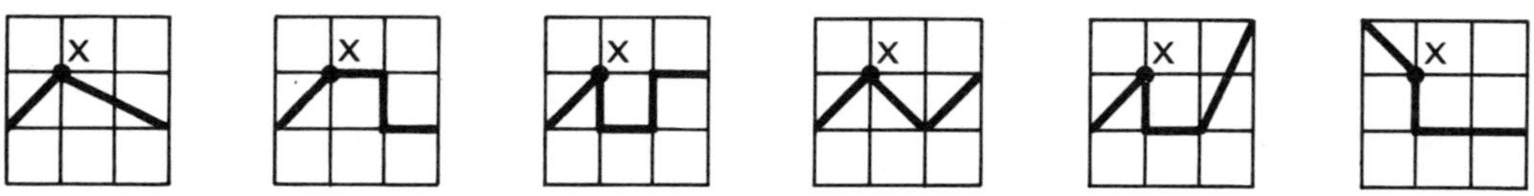

△ Which dissections are possible with one straight line?

△ Try for shapes other than squares.

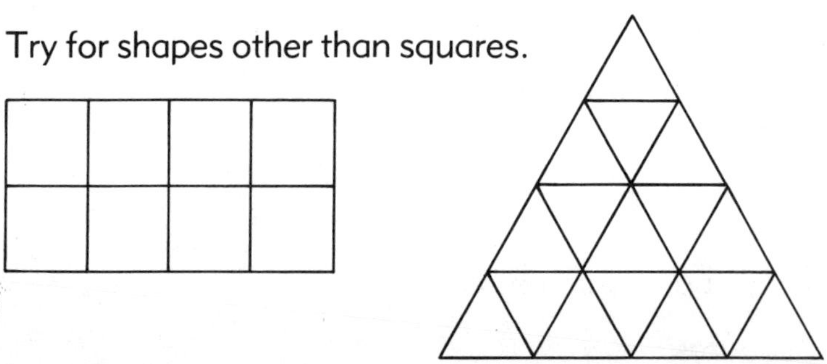

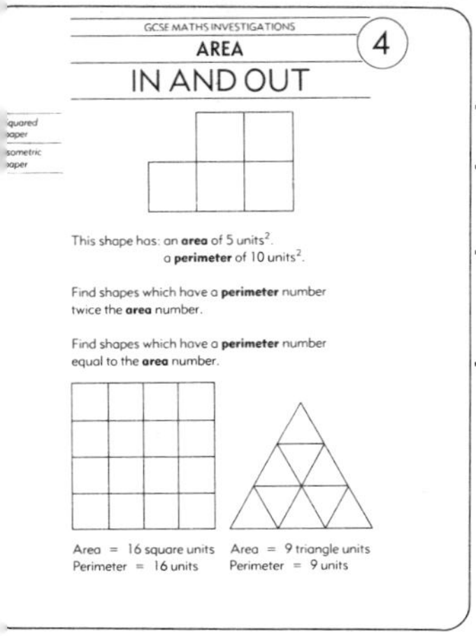
GCSE MATHS INVESTIGATIONS
AREA
IN AND OUT
4

This shape has: an **area** of 5 units^2.
a **perimeter** of 10 units^2.

Find shapes which have a **perimeter** number twice the **area** number.

Find shapes which have a **perimeter** number equal to the **area** number.

Area = 16 square units
Perimeter = 16 units

Area = 9 triangle units
Perimeter = 9 units

GCSE MATHS INVESTIGATIONS

AREA

IN AND OUT

4

Squared paper

Isometric paper

△ Assume integer values for area and perimeter.
One possible approach is to consider shapes drawn within rectangles of known half-perimeter:
e.g.
Try to make shapes where A = 5 and P = 10.
The half-perimeter will be 5.
Possible rectangles are:

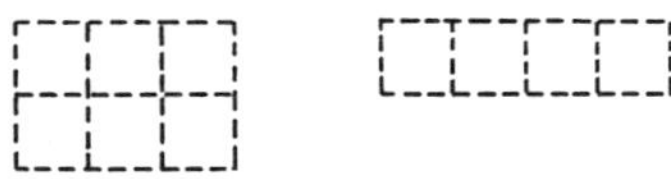

Shapes drawn inside the 2 × 3 rectangle with A = 5 and P = 10 include:

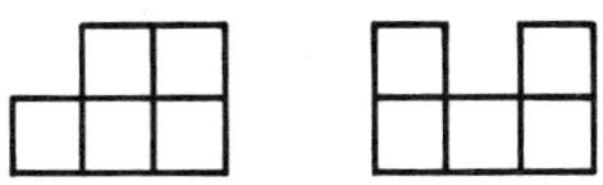

Try A = 6; P = 12.
Possible rectangles with half perimeter of 6 include:

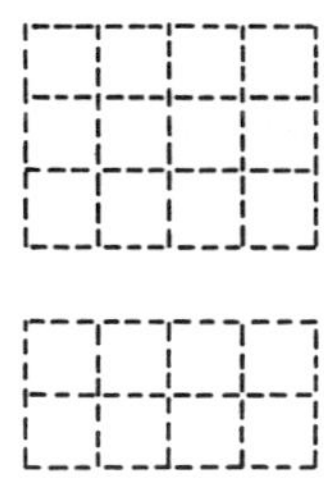

Shapes drawn inside these include:

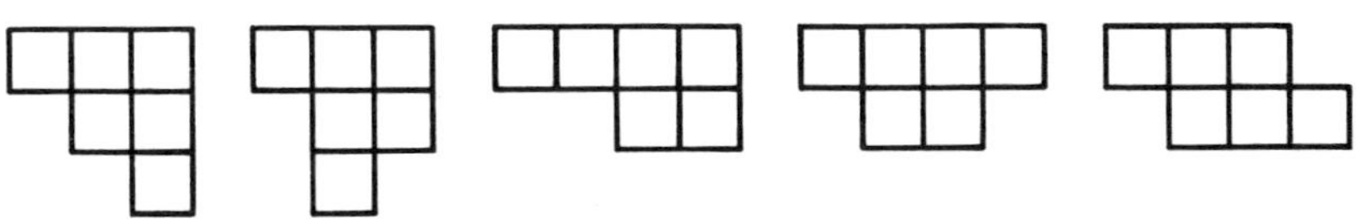

A = 6
P = 12

△ Which rectangles have 2A = P?

△ Some shapes which have area numbers equal to perimeter numbers are:

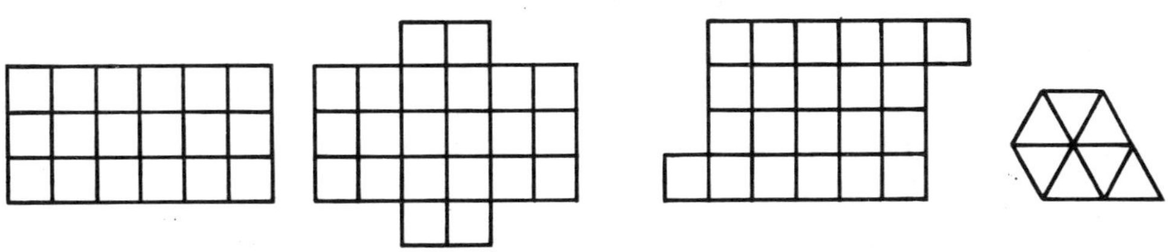

A = 18, P = 18 | A = 22, P = 22 | A = 22, P = 22 | A = 7, P = 7

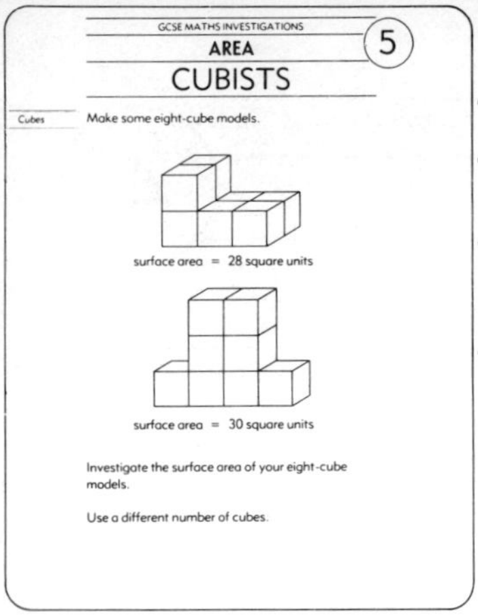
GCSE MATHS INVESTIGATIONS
AREA
CUBISTS
5

Cubes

Make some eight-cube models.

surface area = 28 square units

surface area = 30 square units

Investigate the surface area of your eight-cube models.

Use a different number of cubes.

GCSE MATHS INVESTIGATIONS

AREA

CUBISTS

5

Cubes

△ The minimum and maximum surface areas are:

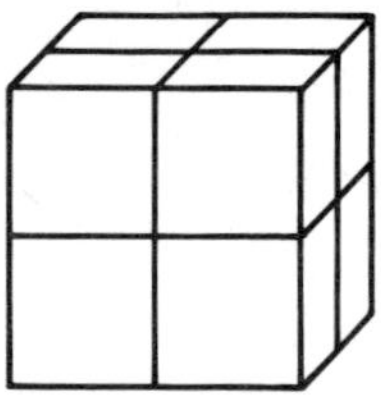

24 square units

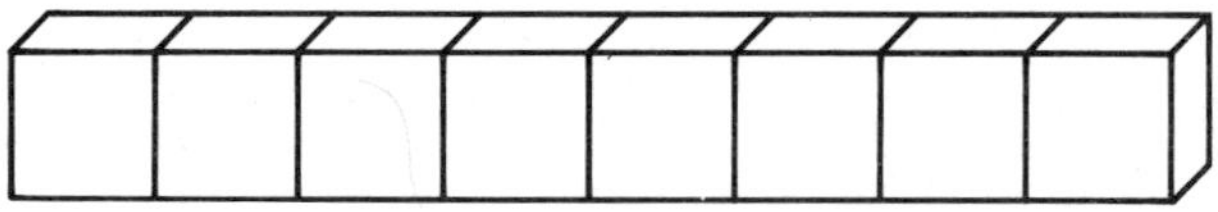

34 square units

△ Several models can have the same surface area.

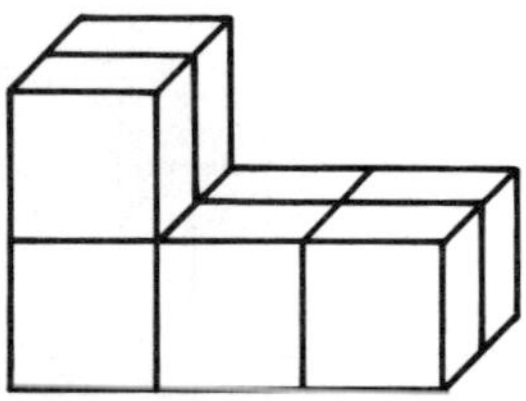

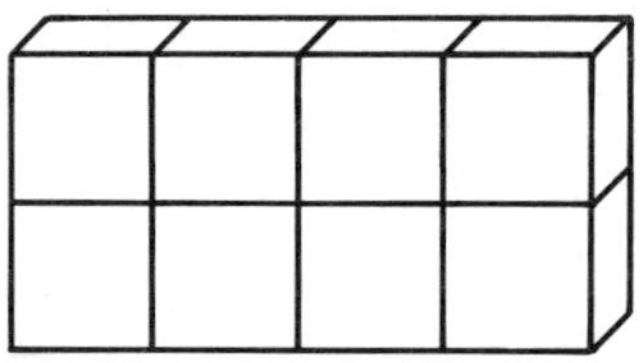

28 square units

△ Find different models which have the same number of cubes on each elevation.

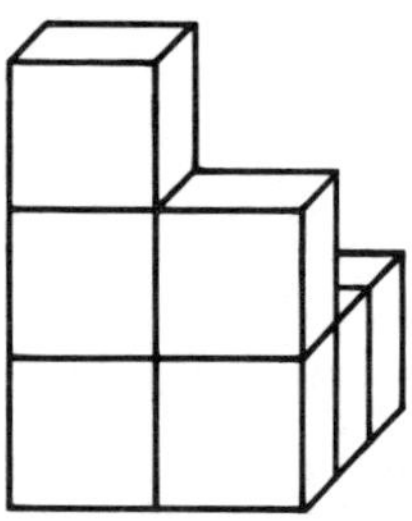

total surface area = 30 square units
each elevation = 5 square units

△ Can a model with a surface area of 26 square units be made?

△ Try making nine-cube models.

△ Which surface areas are not possible?

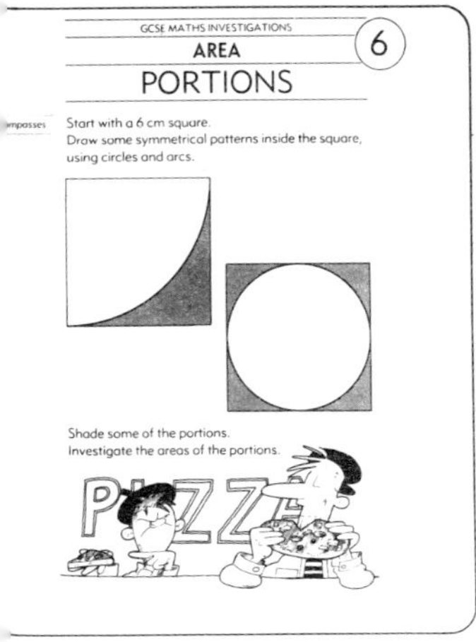

GCSE MATHS INVESTIGATIONS

AREA

PORTIONS

6

Compasses

△ Some possible portions include:

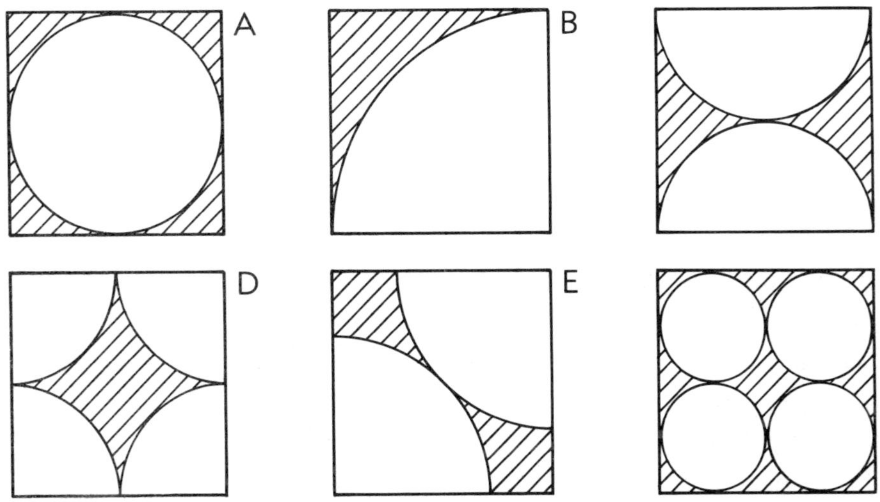

△ The total shaded portion for each shape is $16 - 4\pi$ and the unshaded portion is 4π.

△ Consider each individual portion:

Pattern	Unshaded portion	Shaded portion
A	4π	$4 - \pi$
B	4π	$16 - 4\pi$
C	2π	$8 - 2\pi$
D	π	$16 - 4\pi$
E	2π	$8 - 2\pi$
F	π	$(4 - \pi), \frac{(4 - \pi)}{4}, \frac{(4 - \pi)}{2}$

△ Try with 6 cm equilateral triangles.

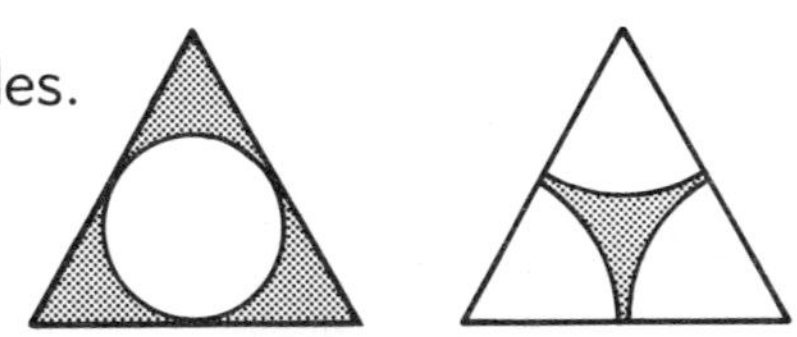

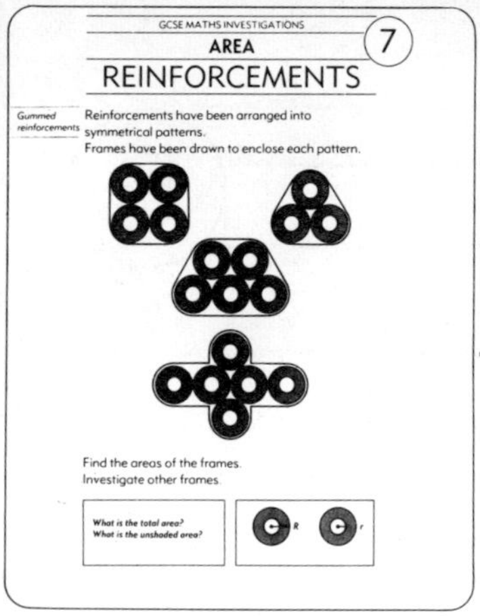
GCSE MATHS INVESTIGATIONS
AREA
REINFORCEMENTS
7
Gummed reinforcements
Reinforcements have been arranged into symmetrical patterns.
Frames have been drawn to enclose each pattern.
Find the areas of the frames.
Investigate other frames.
What is the total area?
What is the unshaded area?

GCSE MATHS INVESTIGATIONS

AREA

REINFORCEMENTS

7

Gummed reinforcements

△ The areas can be considered in terms of the actual dimensions: (outer radius 8mm, inner radius 3 mm) or in terms of R and r.

△

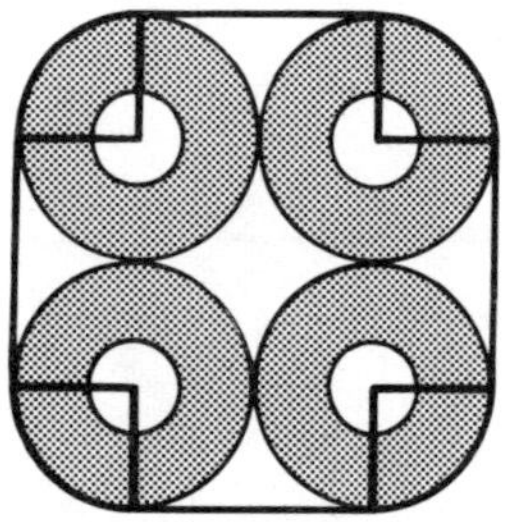

Area of frame = $12R^2 + \pi R^2$
Area of reinforcement = $\pi R^2 - \pi r^2$
Area of unshaded part = $(12R^2 + \pi R^2) - 4(\pi R^2 - \pi r^2)$
$= 12R^2 - 3\pi R^2 + 4\pi r^2$

△ The possible areas between the reinforcements can be considered:

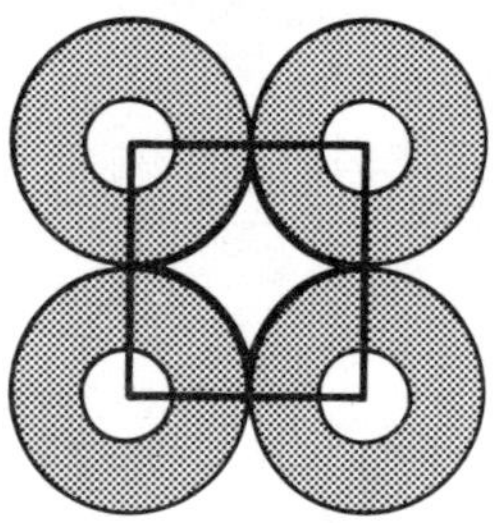

$4R^2 - \pi R^2$

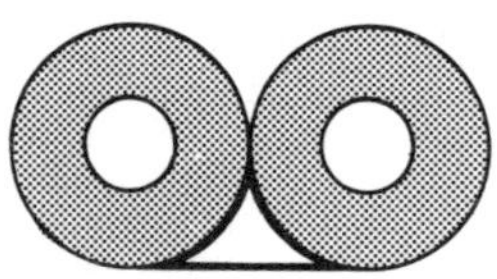

$\frac{1}{2}(4R^2 - \pi R^2)$

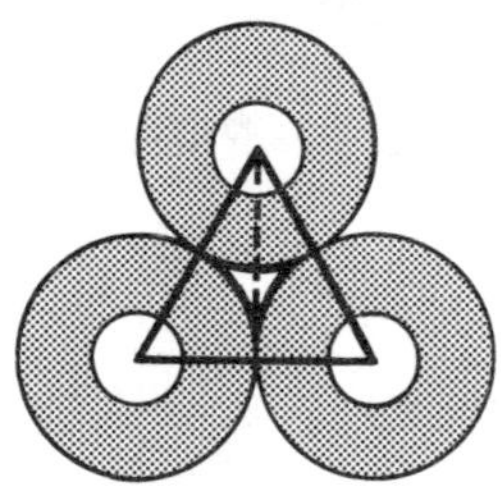

$\sqrt{3R^2 - \frac{\pi R^2}{2}}$

△ Investigate frames which enclose five reinforcements.

△ The use of different gummed shapes makes interesting starting points for investigations.

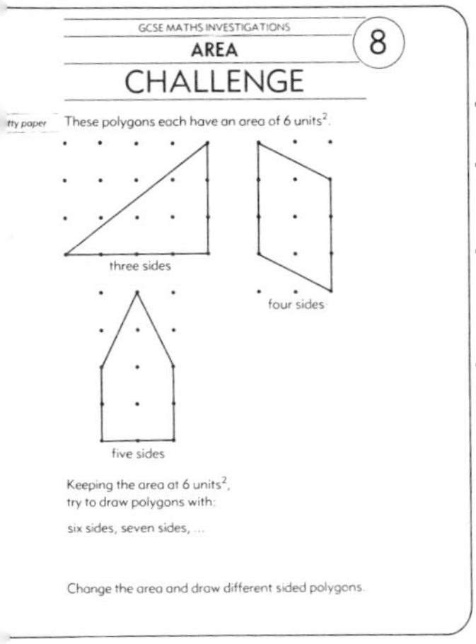
GCSE MATHS INVESTIGATIONS
AREA
CHALLENGE
8
These polygons each have an area of 6 units^2.
three sides
four sides
five sides
Keeping the area at 6 units^2, try to draw polygons with:
six sides, seven sides, ...
Change the area and draw different sided polygons.

GCSE MATHS INVESTIGATIONS

AREA

CHALLENGE

8

Dotty paper

△ Polygons with an area of 6 units^2 include:

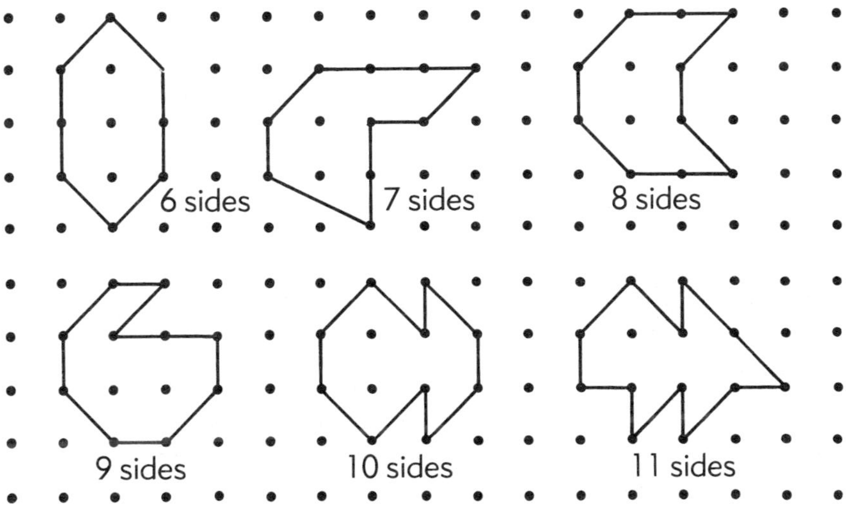

Can a polygon with an area of 6 units^2 and more than 14 sides be drawn?

△ Explore polygons which have a different area.

△ Investigate polygons drawn on isometric dotty paper.
Area of 9 triangle units:

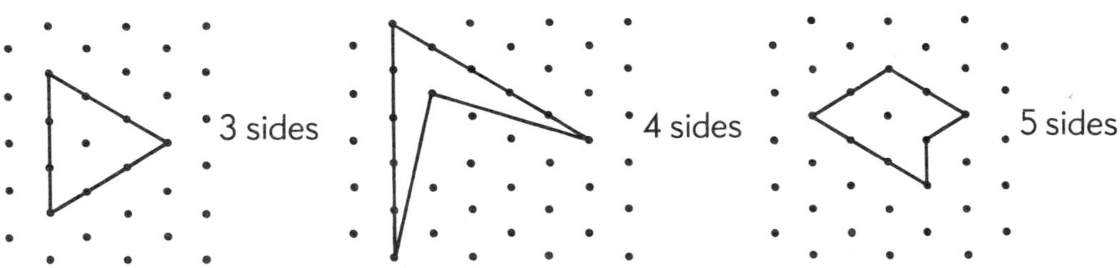

CHAINS

	APPARATUS	ACTIVITY
9 Cycle chains		Cyclic number chains
10 Couples	Calculator	Number patterns produced by multiplication
11 Parents		Adding digits
12 Links		Multiplying digits
13 Dead ends		Cubing digits
14 Flow	Calculator	Flow diagrams. Idea of a limit
15 Chain gang		Squaring digits
16 Square chain		Squaring digit sums

Number chains offer a rich source of investigational material. Many of these activities relate to the digits of a number and operations on them e.g. **squaring, cubing, summing**. It is assumed that pupils will have access to calculators.

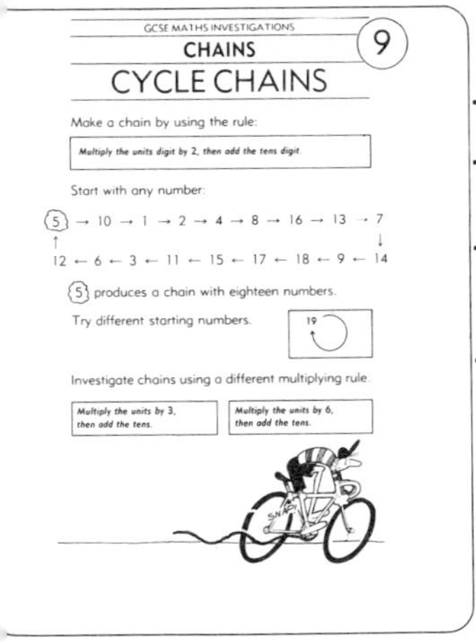
GCSE MATHS INVESTIGATIONS

CHAINS 9

CYCLE CHAINS

Make a chain by using the rule:

Multiply the units digit by 2, then add the tens digit.

Start with any number:

(5) → 10 → 1 → 2 → 4 → 8 → 16 → 13 → 7 ↓

↑ 12 ← 6 ← 3 ← 11 ← 15 ← 17 ← 18 ← 9 ← 14

(5) produces a chain with eighteen numbers.

Try different starting numbers.

19 ↻

Investigate chains using a different multiplying rule.

Multiply the units by 3, then add the tens.

Multiply the units by 6, then add the tens.

GCSE MATHS INVESTIGATIONS

CHAINS

CYCLE CHAINS

9

△ Some discussion may be necessary about the cyclic nature of number chains:

$$\begin{array}{l} \to 5 \to 10 \to 1 \to 2 \to 4 \to 8 \to 16 \to 13 \to 7 \\ 12 \leftarrow 6 \leftarrow 3 \leftarrow 11 \leftarrow 15 \leftarrow 17 \leftarrow 18 \leftarrow 9 \leftarrow 14 \end{array}$$

is the same chain as

$$\begin{array}{l} \to 4 \to 8 \to 16 \to 13 \to 7 \to 14 \to 9 \to 18 \to 17 \\ 2 \leftarrow 1 \leftarrow 10 \leftarrow 5 \leftarrow 12 \leftarrow 6 \leftarrow 3 \leftarrow 11 \leftarrow 15 \end{array}$$

For the general rule: $[k \times \text{units}] + \text{tens} \sim$

△ $\underline{k = 2}$: produces an 18 number chain containing the numbers 1 to 18.
Note that 19 is self-mapping: i.e. 19 ↻
What happens if you start with a number greater than 19?

△ $\underline{k = 3}$: produces a 28 number chain containing the numbers 1 to 28.

$$\begin{array}{l} \to 4 \to 12 \to 7 \to 21 \to 5 \to 15 \to 16 \to 19 \to 28 \\ 8 \leftarrow 22 \leftarrow 17 \leftarrow 25 \leftarrow 18 \leftarrow 6 \leftarrow 2 \leftarrow 20 \leftarrow 26 \\ \to 24 \to 14 \to 13 \to 10 \to 1 \to 3 \to 9 \to 27 \to 23 \\ 11 \end{array}$$

29 is self-mapping: 29 ↻

△ $\underline{k = 4}$: produces six different number chains depending on the starting number.

1 → 4 → 16 → 25 → 22 → 10 (↺ back to 1)

6 → 24 → 18 → 33 → 15 → 21 (↺ back to 6)

2 → 8 → 32 → 11 → 5 → 20 (↺ back to 2)

7 → 28 → 34 → 19 → 37 → 31 (↺ back to 7)

3 → 12 → 9 → 36 → 27 → 30 (↺ back to 3)

14 → 17 → 29 → 38 → 35 → 23 (↺ back to 14)

Self-mapping numbers are: 13, 26 and 39.

△ Which values of k produce a single chain?

△ Investigate self-mapping numbers for different values of k.

△ Investigate the chain lengths for different values of k.

△ Investigate chains produced from different rules:
e.g. $[k \times \text{units}] + [p \times \text{tens}]$

GCSE MATHS INVESTIGATIONS

CHAINS (10)

COUPLES

Calculator

23 → 61 → 27 → 89

This chain is made by **multiplying by** 7 and recording the **last two** digits.

23 × 7 = 161 → 61
61 × 7 = 427 → 27
27 × 7 = 189 → 89
89 × 7 = 623 → 23

Try starting with different numbers.
Investigate **multiplying by** 7 chains.
Investigate other **multiplying** chains.

Multiplying by 3
Multiplying by 9

CHAINS (10)

COUPLES

Calculator

△ 'Multiplying by 7' produces mostly chains of length 4:

1 → 7 → 49 → 43
2 → 14 → 98 → 86
3 → 21 → 47 → 29
4 → 28 → 96 → 72
5 → 35 → 45 → 15
6 → 42 → 94 → 58
8 → 56 → 92 → 44
10 → 70 → 90 → 30

11 → 77 → 73 → 39
12 → 84 → 88 → 16
13 → 91 → 37 → 59
17 → 19 → 33 → 31
18 → 26 → 82 → 74
20 → 40 → 80 → 60
22 → 54 → 78 → 46
23 → 61 → 27 → 89

24 → 68 → 32 → 76
34 → 33 → 62 → 66
36 → 52 → 64 → 48
53 → 71 → 97 → 79
51 → 57 → 99 → 93
65 → 55 → 35 → 45
67 → 69 → 83 → 81
9 → 63 → 41 → 87

Also: 25 → 75   50↻

There are 24 chains of length 4, 1 chain of length 2 and 1 self-mapping number.

△ 'Multiplying by 9' produces mostly chains of length 10:

1 – 9 – 81 – 29 – 61 – 49 – 41 – 69 – 21 – 89
2 – 18 – 62 – 58 – 22 – 98 – 82 – 38 – 42 – 78
3 – 27 – 63 – 17 – 83 – 47 – 23 – 7 – 63 – 67
4 – 36 – 24 – 16 – 44 – 96 – 64 – 76 – 84 – 56
6 – 54 – 86 – 74 – 66 – 94 – 46 – 14 – 26 – 34
8 – 72 – 48 – 32 – 88 – 92 – 28 – 52 – 68 – 12
11 – 99 – 91 – 19 – 71 – 39 – 51 – 59 – 31 – 79
13 – 17 – 53 – 77 – 93 – 37 – 33 – 97 – 73 – 57

and 25↻   50↻   75↻

Also:

5 → 45
10 → 90
15 → 35
20 → 80

55 → 95
65 → 85
30 → 70
40 → 60

There are 8 chains of length 10, 8 chains of length 2 and 3 self-mapping numbers.

△ 'Multiplying by 3' produces 4 chains of length 20 and 4 chains of length 4.
Is it possible to predict what will happen for a given multiplier?

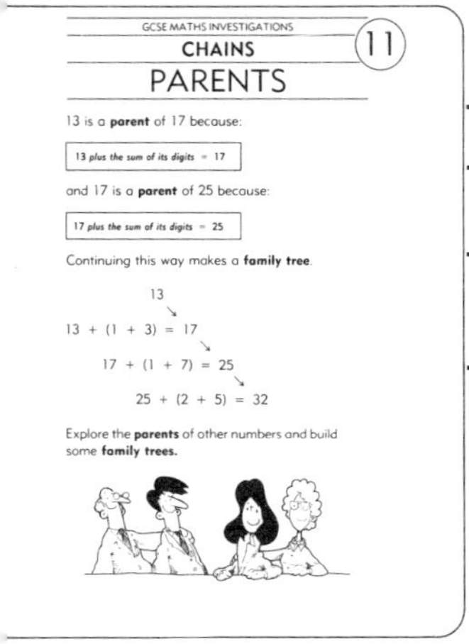

GCSE MATHS INVESTIGATIONS

CHAINS (11)

PARENTS

13 is a **parent** of 17 because:

13 plus the sum of its digits = 17

and 17 is a **parent** of 25 because:

17 plus the sum of its digits = 25

Continuing this way makes a **family tree**.

13 ↘

13 + (1 + 3) = 17 ↘

17 + (1 + 7) = 25 ↘

25 + (2 + 5) = 32

Explore the **parents** of other numbers and build some **family trees.**

GCSE MATHS INVESTIGATIONS

CHAINS (11)

PARENTS

△ Here is one example of several different family trees which can be found:

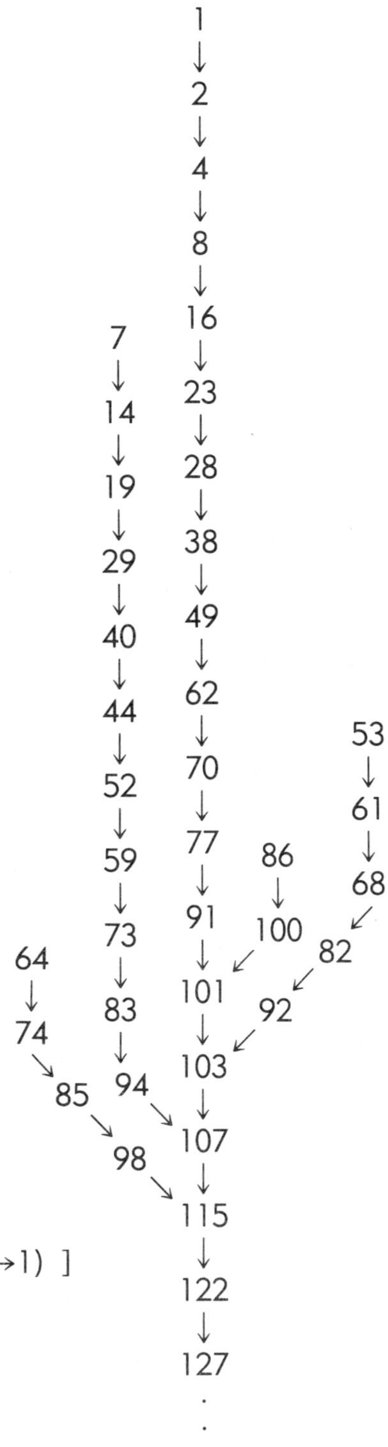

△ Which numbers have no parents? These are **orphan numbers**. The orphan numbers less than 100 include: 1, 3, 5, 7, 9, 20, 31, 42, 53, 64, 75, 86, 97.

△ Which numbers have two parents? For example:

107 ↘ 115 ↙ 98

92 ↘ 103 ↙ 101

Numbers with two parents include: 101, 103, 105, 107, 109, 111, 113, 115, ...

△ It is interesting to explore the "digital roots" of the numbers in the family trees.

[To find the digital root: sum the digits, continuing if necessary until a single-digit is arrived at: e.g.
digital root of 52 is 7 (5 + 2 → 7)
digital root of 73 is 1 (7 + 3 → 10, 1 + 0 → 1)]

△ The digital roots of the numbers in the family tree illustrated produce the following repeated pattern: 1 → 2 → 4 → 8 → 7 → 5

GCSE MATHS INVESTIGATIONS

CHAINS (12)

LINKS

Choose a starting number.
Multiply the digits together.
Continue until you obtain a single-digit number.

67 → 42 → 8
(6 × 7) (4 × 2)
two links ending in 8

47 → 28 → 16 → 6
(4 × 7) (2 × 8) (1 × 6)
three links ending in 6

Try for other starting numbers.
Which starting numbers end in 6?
Which starting numbers make chains with three links?

GCSE MATHS INVESTIGATIONS

CHAINS (12)

LINKS

△ One approach is to consider the starting number in sequence. Some examples include:

41 → 4
42 → 8
43 → 12 → 2
44 → 16 → 6
45 → 20 → 0
46 → 24 → 8
47 → 28 → 16 → 6
48 → 32 → 6
49 → 36 → 18 → 8
50 → 0

51 → 5
52 → 10 → 0
53 → 15 → 5
54 → 20 → 0
55 → 25 → 10 → 0
56 → 30 → 0
57 → 35 → 15 → 5
58 → 40 → 0
59 → 45 → 20 → 0
60 → 0

61 → 6
62 → 12 → 2
63 → 18 → 8
64 → 24 → 8
65 → 30 → 0
66 → 36 → 18 → 8
67 → 42 → 8
68 → 48 → 32 → 6
69 → 54 → 20 → 0
70 → 0

△ Consider the end digit in the chain for different starting numbers.

End digit of chain	*Starting numbers*
0	10, 20, 30, 40, 50, 60, 70, 80, 90, 25, 45, 55, 65, 85, 95, 52, 54, 56, 58, 69, 78, 87, 96, 59
1	11
2	12, 21, 26, 34, 37, 43, 62, 73
3	13, 31
4	14, 22, 27, 39, 41, 72, 89, 93, 98
5	15, 35, 51, 53, 57, 75
6	16, 23, 28, 32, 44, 47, 48, 61, 68, 74, 82, 84, 86
7	17, 71
8	18, 24, 29, 36, 38, 42, 46, 49, 63, 64, 66, 67, 76, 77, 79, 81, 83, 88, 92, 94, 97, 99
9	19, 91

Which starting numbers end in an odd number?

△ Three link chains are produced by the following starting numbers: 39, 47, 49, 55, 57, 59, ...

△ One example of a four link chain is: 77 → 49 → 36 → 18 → 8
Are there any more?

△ Suppose the starting number has three digits? 299 → 162 → 12 → 2

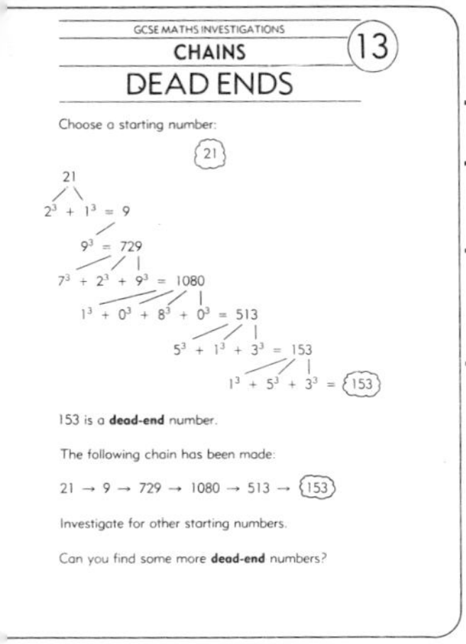
GCSE MATHS INVESTIGATIONS

CHAINS 13

DEAD ENDS

Choose a starting number:

21

$2^3 + 1^3 = 9$

$9^3 = 729$

$7^3 + 2^3 + 9^3 = 1080$

$1^3 + 0^3 + 8^3 + 0^3 = 513$

$5^3 + 1^3 + 3^3 = 153$

$1^3 + 5^3 + 3^3 = 153$

153 is a **dead-end** number.

The following chain has been made:

21 → 9 → 729 → 1080 → 513 → 153

Investigate for other starting numbers.

Can you find some more **dead-end** numbers?

CHAINS 13

DEAD ENDS

△ A table of the cubes of digits 1 to 9 is helpful.

1^3	2^3	3^3	4^3	5^3	6^3	7^3	8^3	9^3
1	8	27	64	125	216	343	512	729

△ Several chains can be found. One example is:

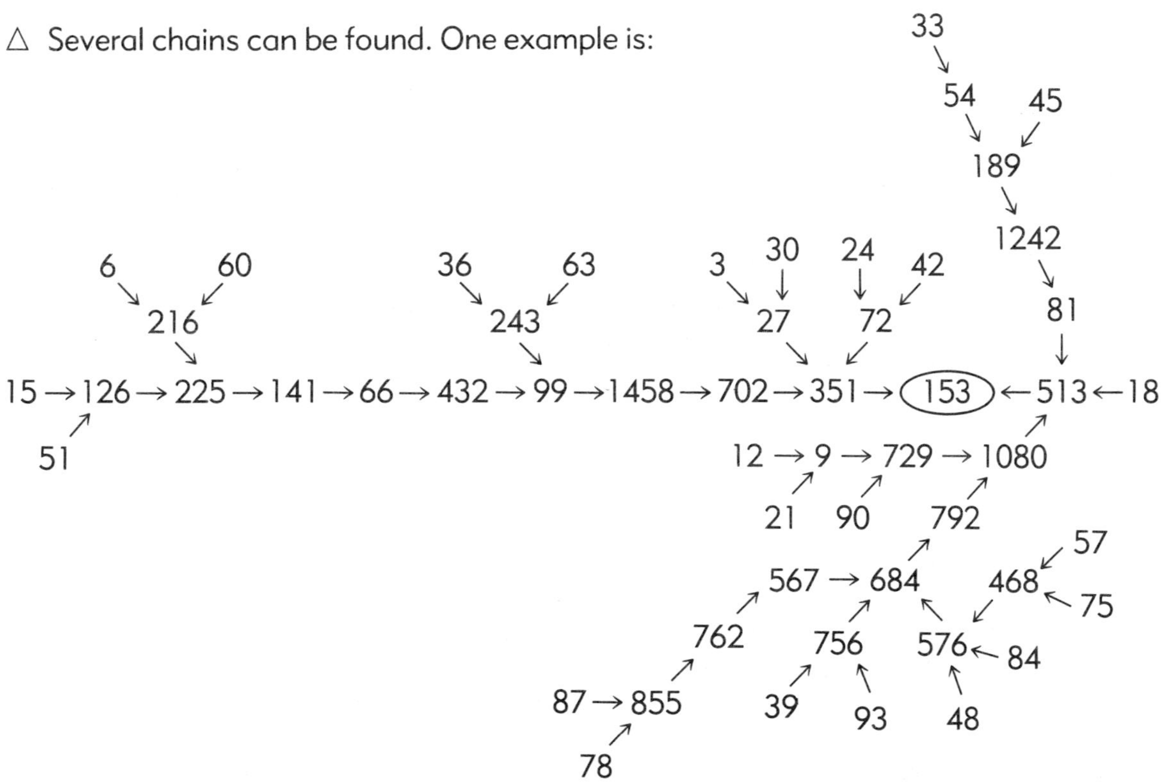

△ Some chains contain a loop.

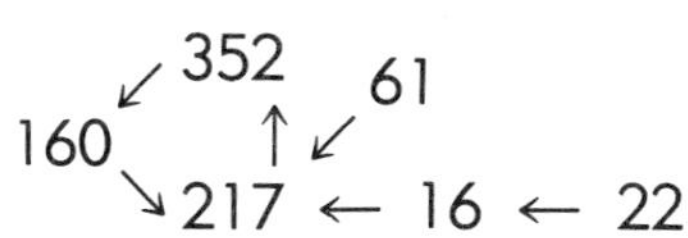

△ Dead-end numbers include: 153, 371, 370, 407, ...

△ Investigate chains produced by different rules.
e.g. Sum the squares of the digits instead of the cubes.

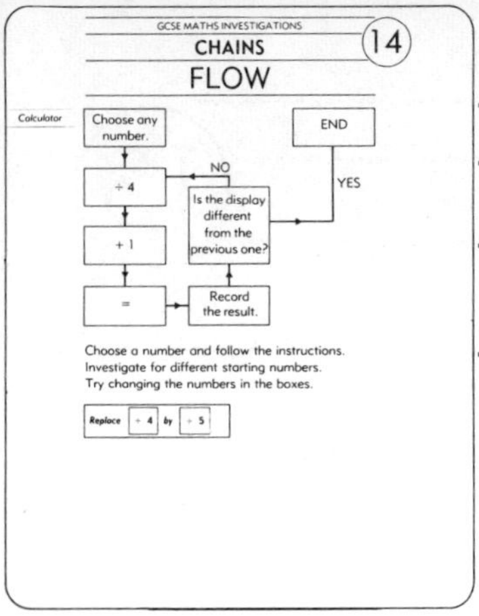

GCSE MATHS INVESTIGATIONS

CHAINS

FLOW

14

Calculator

△ The chain x [÷4] [+1] [=]

eventually displays 1.3333333. $(1\frac{1}{3})$

The chain x [÷5] [+1] [=]

eventually displays 1.25. $(1\frac{1}{4})$

The chain x [÷6] [+1] [=]

eventually displays 1.999999 (1.2 on some calculators). $(1\frac{1}{5})$

Hence, x [÷ n] [+1] [=] will eventually display the decimal equivalent of $1\frac{1}{(n-1)}$.

△ Change the addition constant.

x [÷4] [+3] [=] eventually displays 3.9999999.

x [÷5] [+3] [=] eventually displays 3.7499999. (3.75)

Hence, x [÷ n] [+ p] will eventually display the decimal equivalent

of $p + \frac{p}{(n-1)}$.

△ Investigate different operations in the flow diagram.

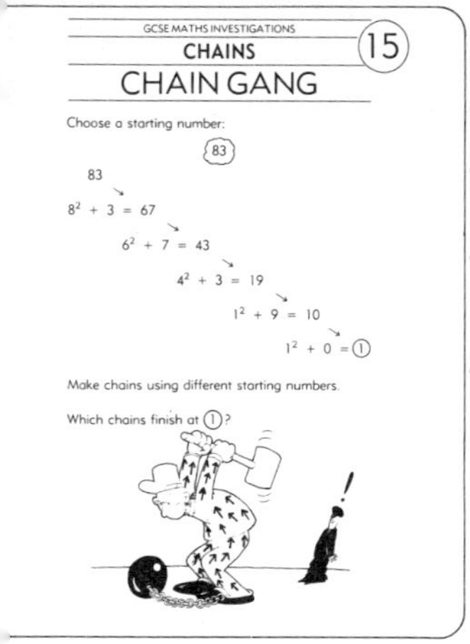
GCSE MATHS INVESTIGATIONS
CHAINS
CHAIN GANG
15

Choose a starting number: (83)

83

$8^2 + 3 = 67$

$6^2 + 7 = 43$

$4^2 + 3 = 19$

$1^2 + 9 = 10$

$1^2 + 0 =$ (1)

Make chains using different starting numbers.

Which chains finish at (1)?

CHAIN GANG

△ One approach is to choose a set of starting numbers in sequence:

50 → 25 → 9	60 → 36 → 15 → 6
51 → 26 → 10 → 1	61 → 37 → 16 → 7
52 → 27 → 11 → 2	62 → 38 → 17 → 8
53 → 28 → 12 → 3	63 → 39 → 18 → 9
54 → 29 → 13 → 4	64 → 40 → 16 → 7
55 → 30 → 9	65 → 41 → 17 → 8
56 → 31 → 10 → 1	66 → 42 → 18 → 9
57 → 32 → 11 → 2	67 → 43 → 19 → 10 → 1
58 → 33 → 12 → 3	68 → 44 → 20 → 4
59 → 34 → 13 → 4	69 → 45 → 21 → 5

△ Chains can end in the digits 1 to 9.
Consider two-digit starting numbers. Some examples of linked chains include:

92 → 83 → 67 → 43 → 19 ↘
97 → 88 → 72 → 51 → 26 → 10 → (1)
77 → 56 → 31 ↗

47 → 23 ↘
61 → 37 → 16 → (7)
80 → 64 → 40 ↗

93 → 84 → 68 → 44 → 20 → (4)
75 → 54 → 29 → 13 ↗
59 → 34 ↗

98 → 89 → 73 → 52 → 27 → 11 → (2)
78 → 57 → 32 ↗

△ Three numbers link to 9:

30 ↘
18 → (9)
25 ↗

Are there other numbers having three linking numbers?

△ Investigate similar rules for making chains: $83 \rightarrow 8^2 - 3 = 61$

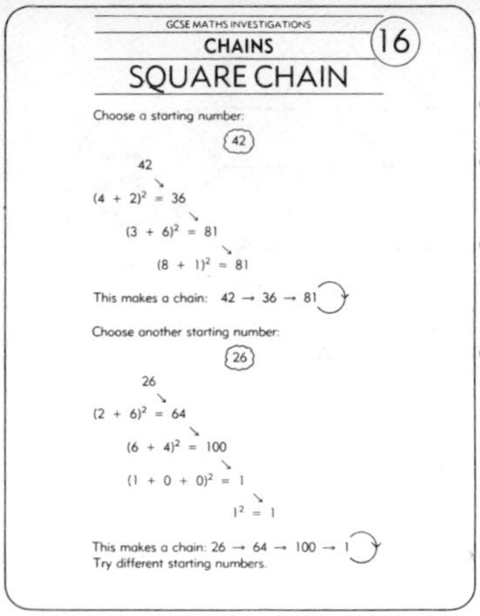
GCSE MATHS INVESTIGATIONS

CHAINS 16

SQUARE CHAIN

Choose a starting number:

(42)

42

$(4 + 2)^2 = 36$

$(3 + 6)^2 = 81$

$(8 + 1)^2 = 81$

This makes a chain: 42 → 36 → 81 ↻

Choose another starting number:

(26)

26

$(2 + 6)^2 = 64$

$(6 + 4)^2 = 100$

$(1 + 0 + 0)^2 = 1$

$1^2 = 1$

This makes a chain: 26 → 64 → 100 → 1 ↻

Try different starting numbers.

CHAINS

SQUARE CHAIN

△ Consider single and two-digit numbers:
Numbers whose digits sum to 5 will link to 5^2 → 25.
These are 5, 50, 14, 41, 23, 32.

A: 2, 20, 11 → 4

B: 3, 30, 12, 21 → 9

C: 4, 40, 13, 31, 22 → 16

D: 5, 50, 14, 41, 23, 32 → 25

E: 6, 60, 15, 51, 24, 42, 33 → 36

F: 7, 70, 16, 61, 25, 52, 34, 43 → 49

G: 8, 80, 17, 71, 26, 62, 35, 53, 44 → 64

H: 9, 90, 18, 81, 27, 72, 36, 63, 45, 54 → 81

I: 19, 91, 28, 82, 37, 73, 46, 64, 55 → 100

J: 92, 29, 83, 38, 74, 47, 65, 56 → 121

K: 93, 39, 84, 48, 75, 57, 66 → 144

L: 94, 49, 85, 58, 76, 67 → 169

M: 95, 59, 86, 68, 77 → 196

N: 96, 69, 87, 78 → 225

P: 97, 79, 88 → 256

Q: 98, 89 → 289

△ These numbers can be linked to chains in sets.

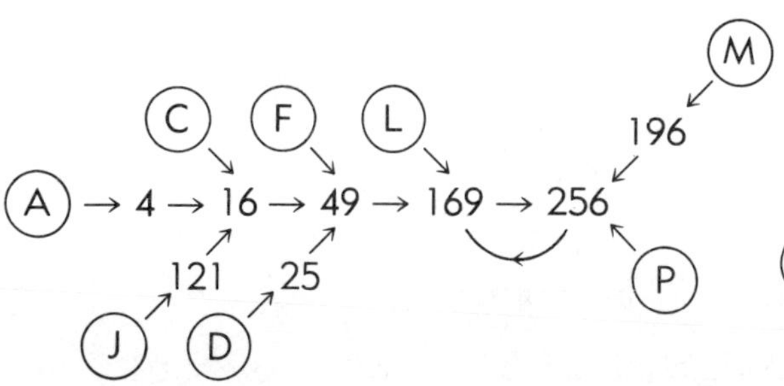

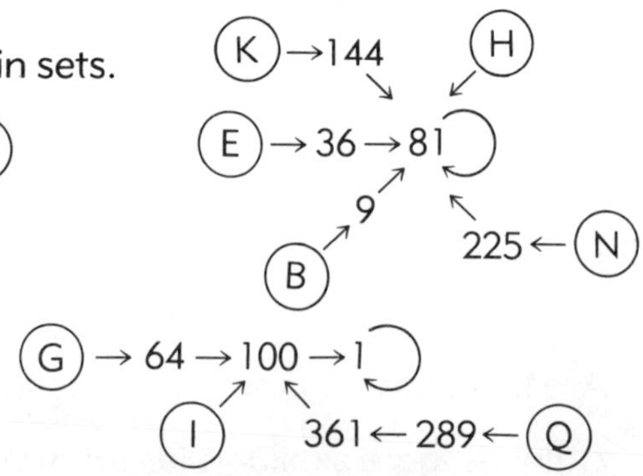

HEXAGONS

	APPARATUS	ACTIVITY
17 Hexashapes		Shapes formed by the diagonals of polygons
18 Hexplode		Dividing a hexagon into equal pieces
19 Hexchange	Geoboard Dotty paper Elastic bands	Producing different geoboard hexagons
20 Trisquare	Card Scissors	Tessellation
21 Hextra	Dotty paper	Drawing and classifying different hexagons. Perimeters
22 Hexahunt	Dotty paper	Drawing hexagons on 3×3 grids
23 Reflexions		Drawing hexagons containing reflex angles
24 Hexasizes	Isometric dotty paper	Hexagonal numbers

The theme of hexagons provides a starting point for activities based on a variety of geometrical ideas e.g. tessellation, symmetry, angle.

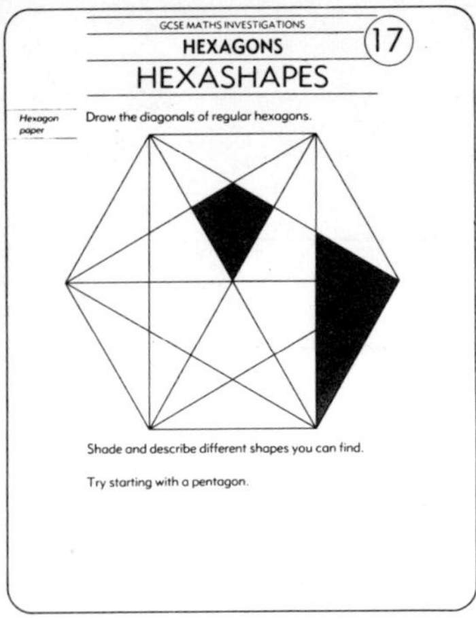
GCSE MATHS INVESTIGATIONS
HEXAGONS
HEXASHAPES
Hexagon paper
Draw the diagonals of regular hexagons.
Shade and describe different shapes you can find.
Try starting with a pentagon.

GCSE MATHS INVESTIGATIONS

HEXAGONS

HEXASHAPES

Hexagon paper

△ One strategy is to start looking for triangles.
Some possibilities include:

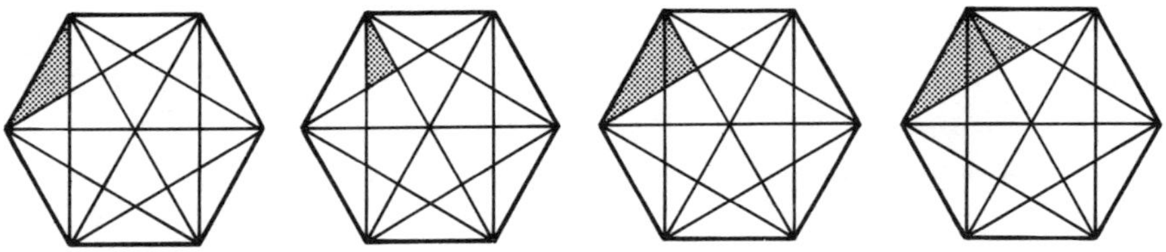

isosceles | right-angled | right-angled | right-angled

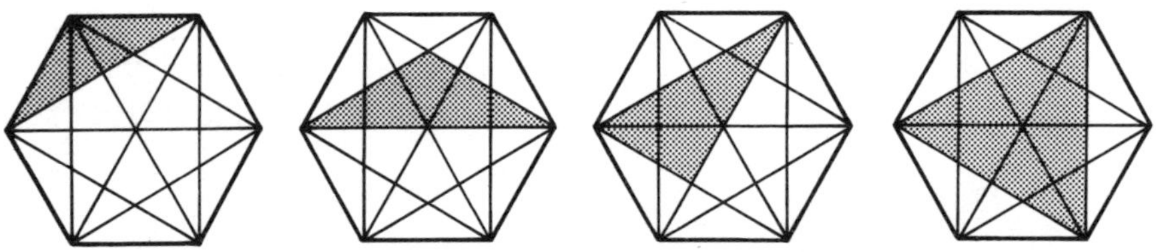

isosceles | isosceles | right-angled | equilateral

△ The next stage may be to look for quadrilaterals:

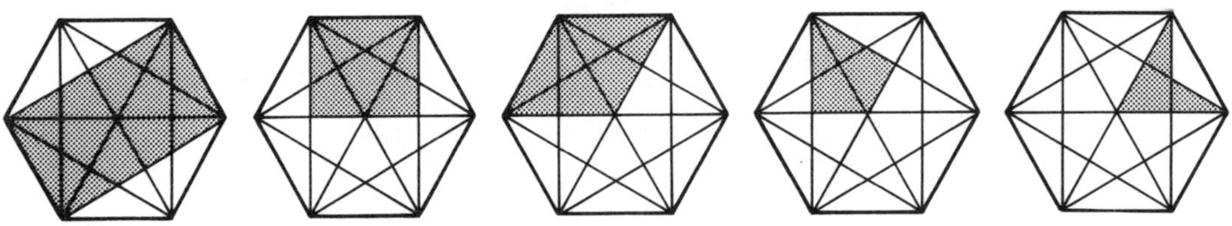

rectangle | square | rhombus | kite | arrowhead

Then other shapes can be investigated such as pentagons, hexagons.

△ Pupils should be encouraged to name the shapes as fully as possible.

△ Investigate the angles of the shapes.

△ The activity can be extended by starting with other regular polygons and drawing the diagonals.

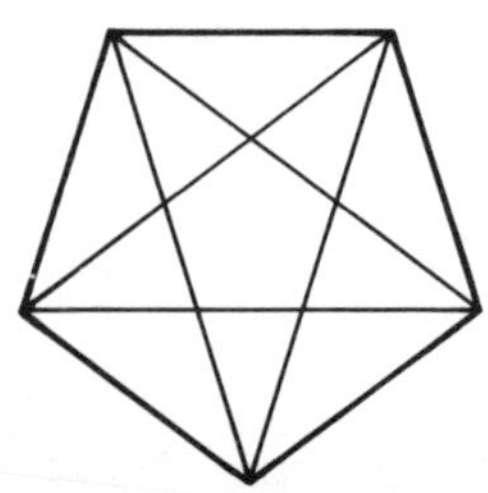

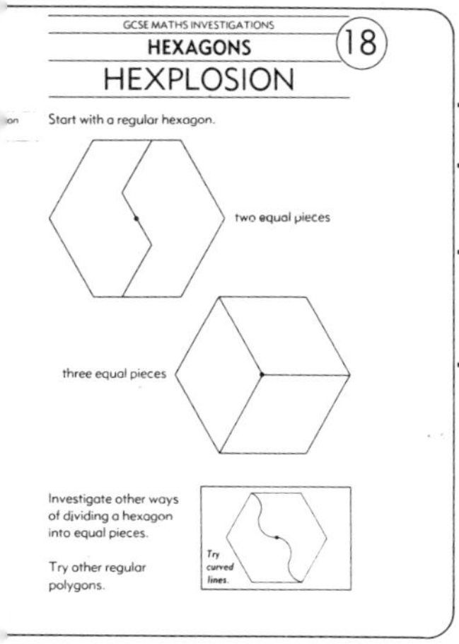

GCSE MATHS INVESTIGATIONS

HEXAGONS

18

HEXPLOSIONS

Hexagon paper

△ Two equal pieces:

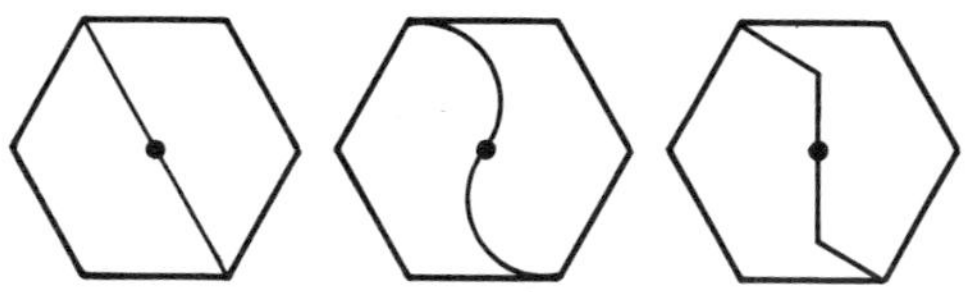

type A

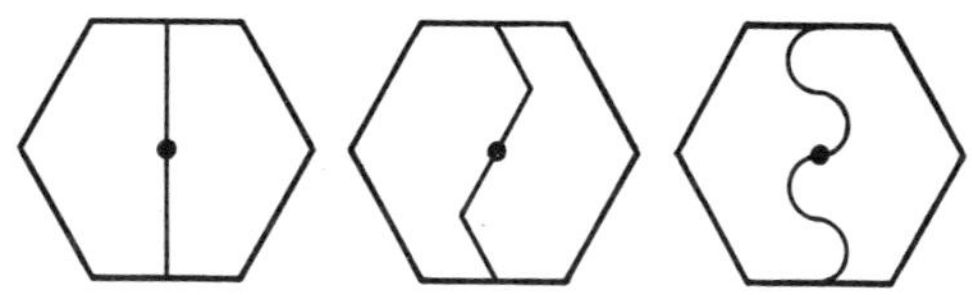

type B

△ Three equal pieces:

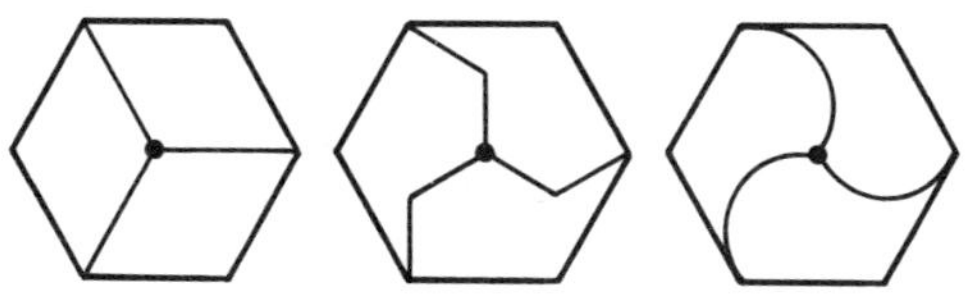

type A

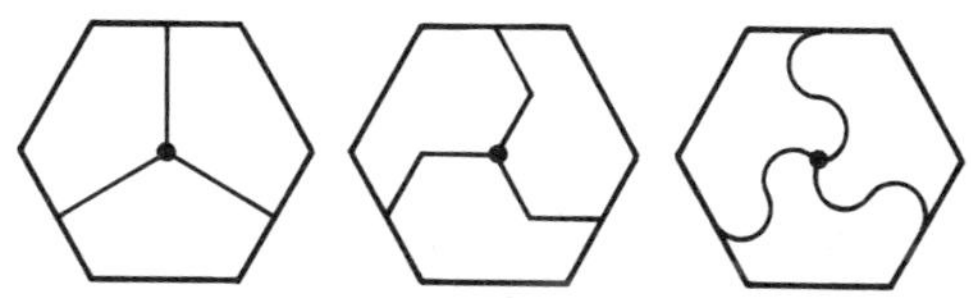

type B

△ Four equal pieces:

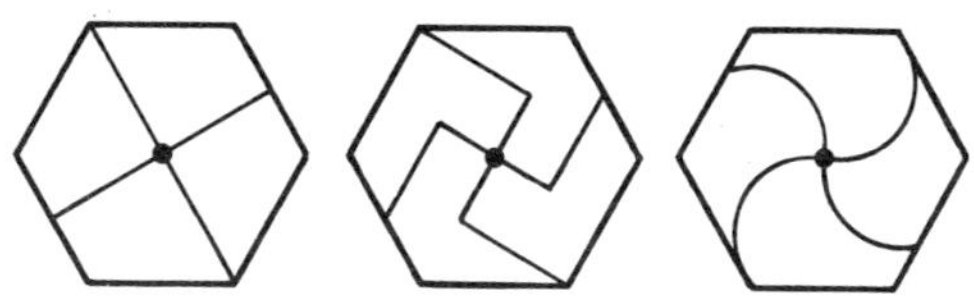

△ Explore the order of rotational symmetry for each shape.

△ Can hexagons be divided equally into other pieces?

△ Can a hexagon be divided into five congruent parts?

△ Look at divisions which produce symmetrical parts.

△ Try dividing other regular polygons.

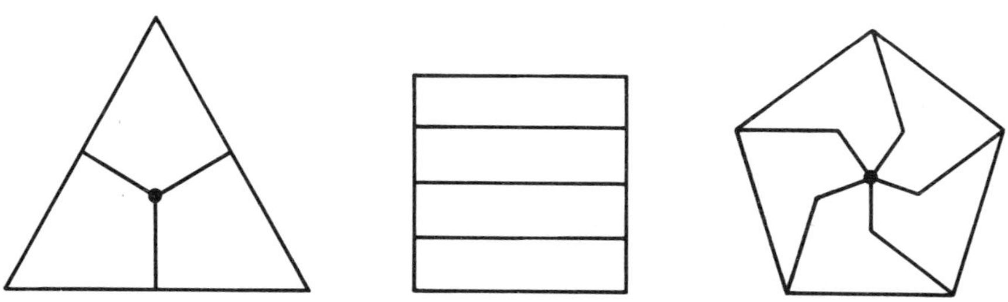

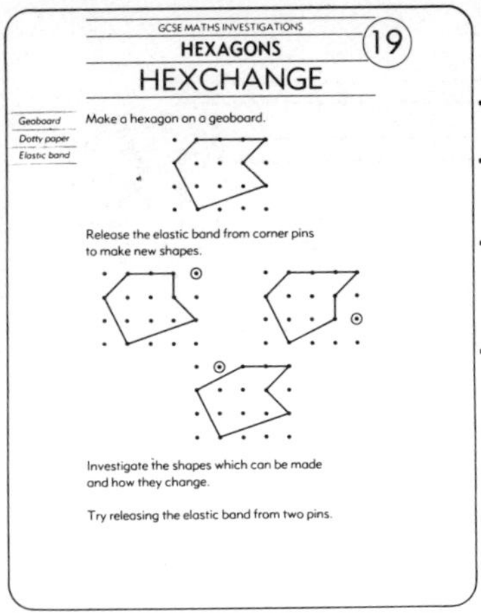
GCSE MATHS INVESTIGATIONS

HEXAGONS (19)

HEXCHANGE

Geoboard
Dotty paper
Elastic band

Make a hexagon on a geoboard.

Release the elastic band from corner pins to make new shapes.

Investigate the shapes which can be made and how they change.

Try releasing the elastic band from two pins.

HEXAGONS (19)

HEXCHANGE

Geoboard
Elastic bands
Dotty paper

△ If the pins are numbered and considered in turn, the resulting shapes can be studied.

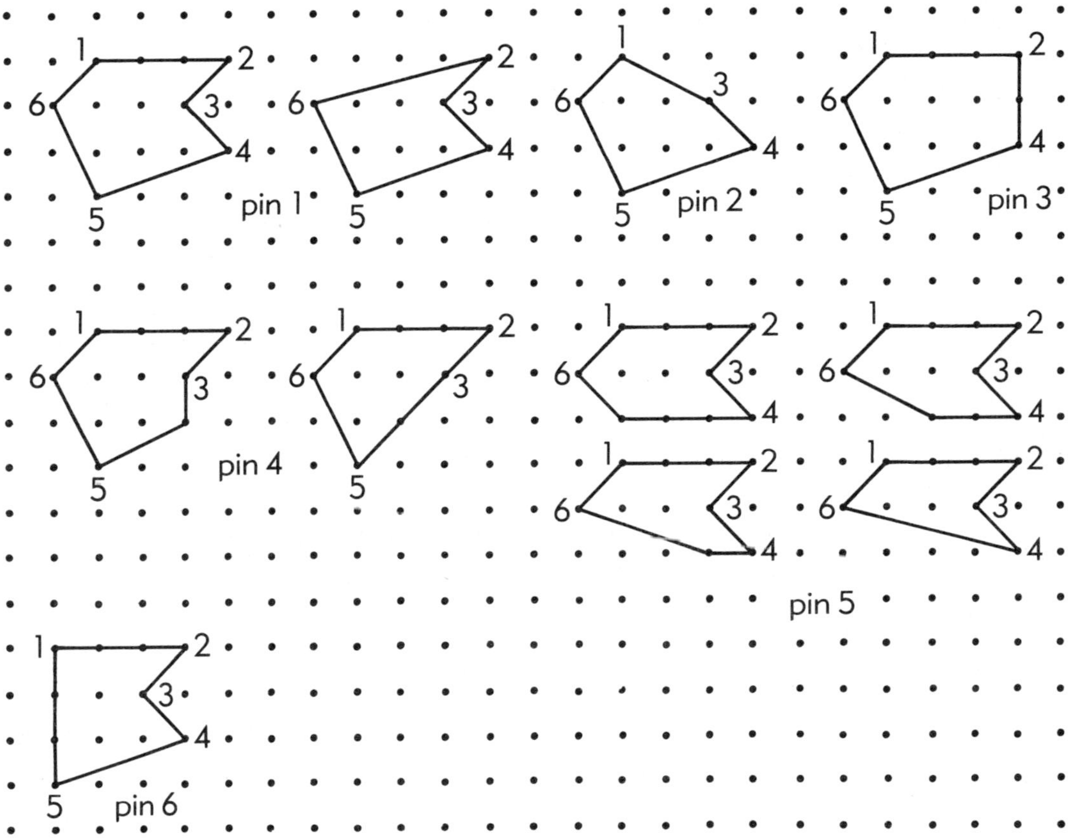

Try releasing two pins.

△ Which pins need to be released to make a triangle? square? rectangle?

△ Try releasing pins to maintain a hexagon.

△ Release pins to make each successive polygon have fewer sides.

△ Areas and perimeters of the shapes can be investigated.

△ Start with a different polygon.

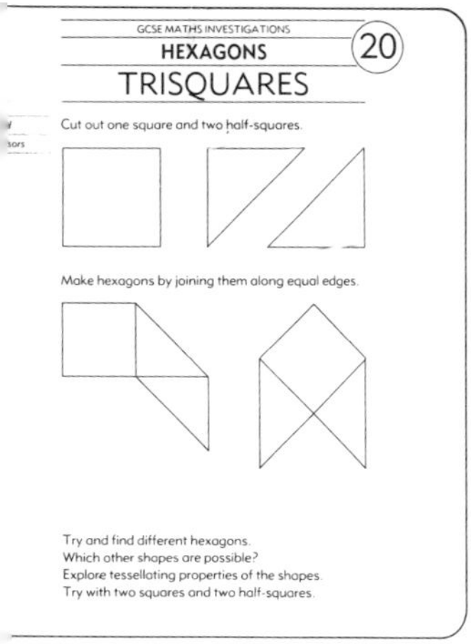
GCSE MATHS INVESTIGATIONS
HEXAGONS
TRISQUARES
20

Cut out one square and two half-squares.

Make hexagons by joining them along equal edges.

Try and find different hexagons.
Which other shapes are possible?
Explore tessellating properties of the shapes.
Try with two squares and two half-squares.

GCSE MATHS INVESTIGATIONS

HEXAGONS

TRISQUARES

20

Card
Scissors

△ Hexagons with one square and two halves.

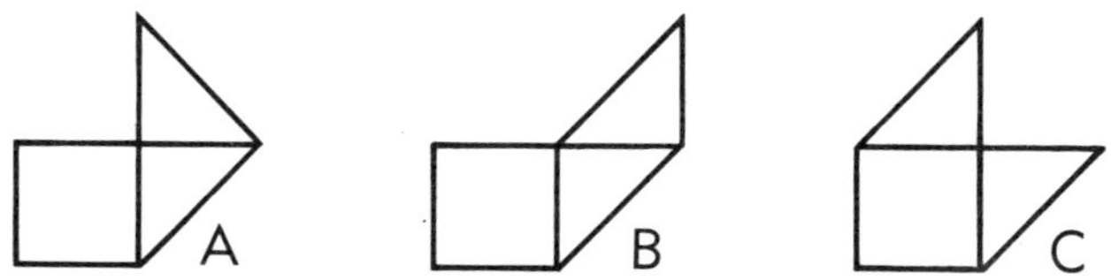

Each hexagon tessellates.
Hexagon A makes a "hexagon" tessellation.

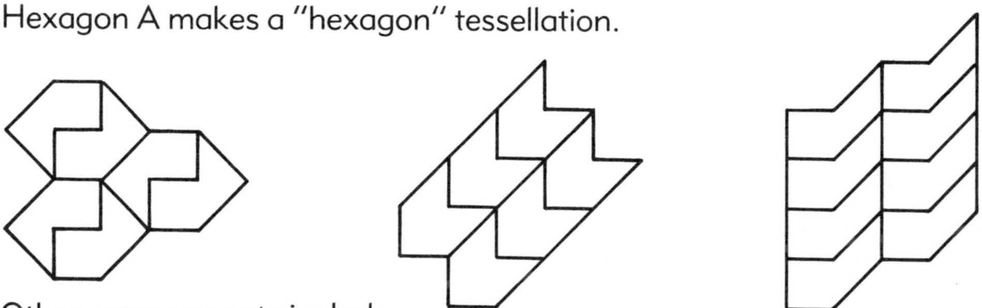

△ Other arrangements include:

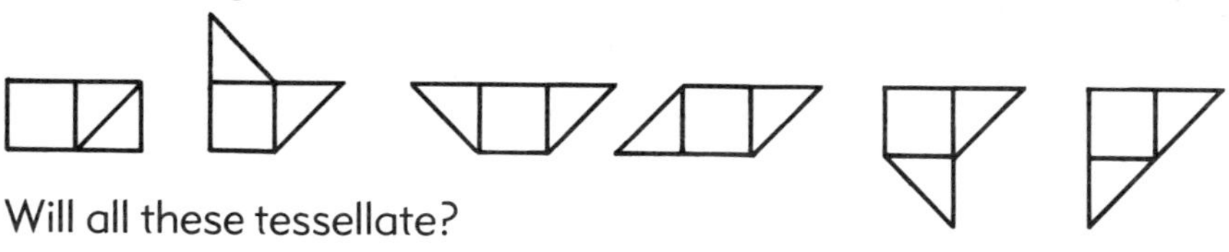

Will all these tessellate?

△ Look at two squares and two halves. Hexagons:

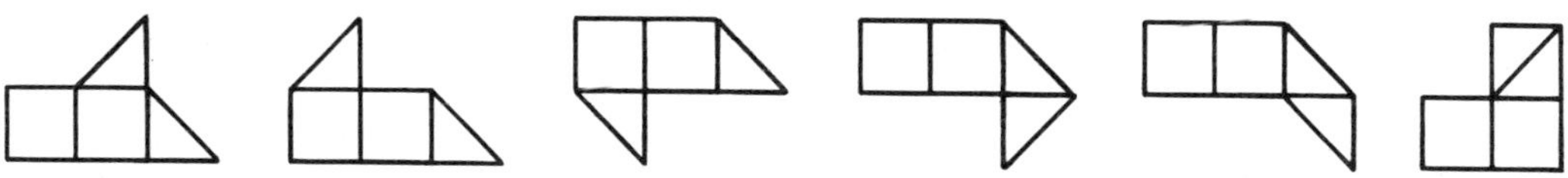

Others include:

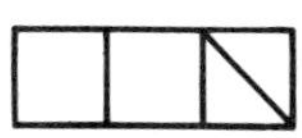

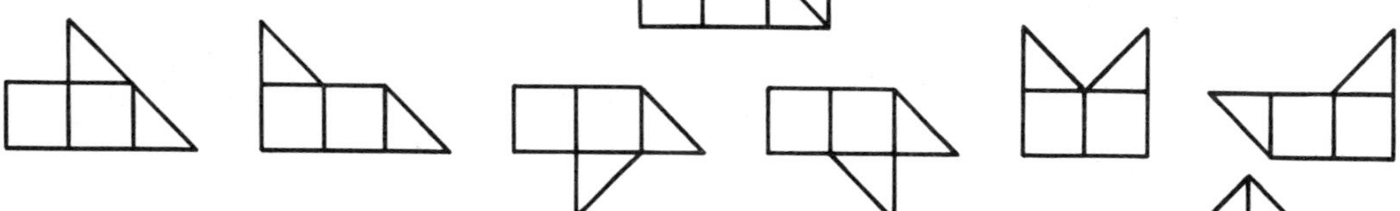

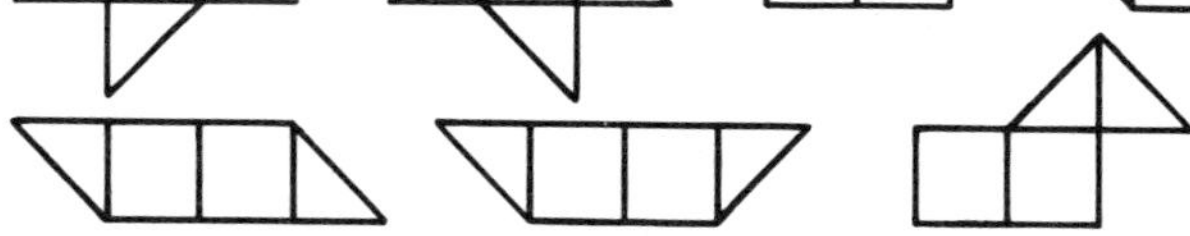

Will they all tessellate?

△ Try other combinations of squares and halves.

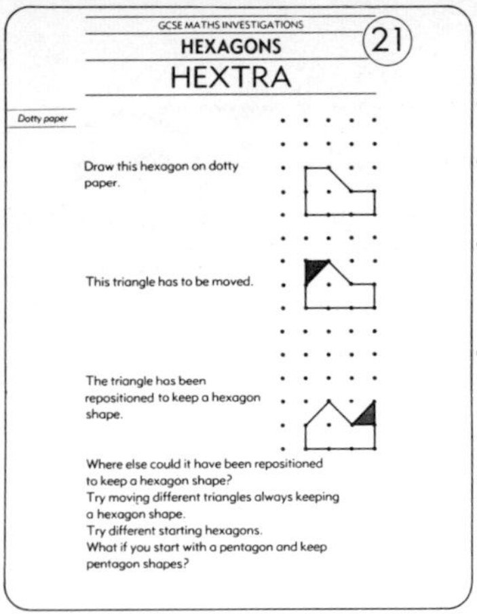
GCSE MATHS INVESTIGATIONS
HEXAGONS
21
HEXTRA
Dotty paper
Draw this hexagon on dotty paper.
This triangle has to be moved.
The triangle has been repositioned to keep a hexagon shape.
Where else could it have been repositioned to keep a hexagon shape?
Try moving different triangles always keeping a hexagon shape.
Try different starting hexagons.
What if you start with a pentagon and keep pentagon shapes?

HEXAGONS

HEXTRA

Dotty paper

△ The shaded triangle to be moved:

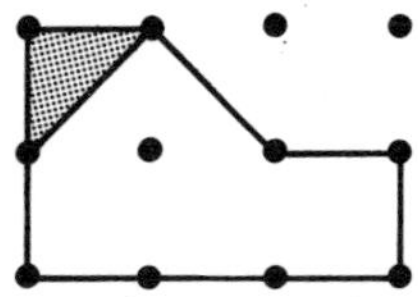

Some possibilities:

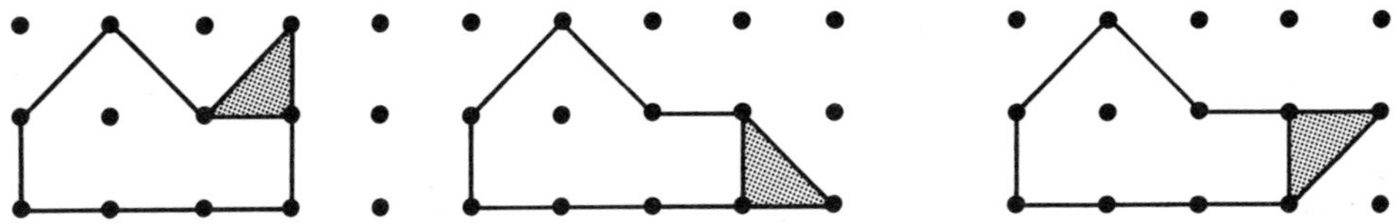

Are there any more?

△ Consider a different triangle to move:

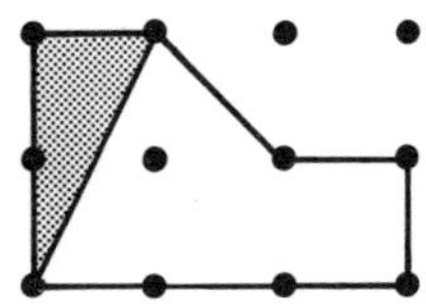

△ Which starting hexagon produces most possibilites?

△ Hexagon chains can be made by moving triangles:

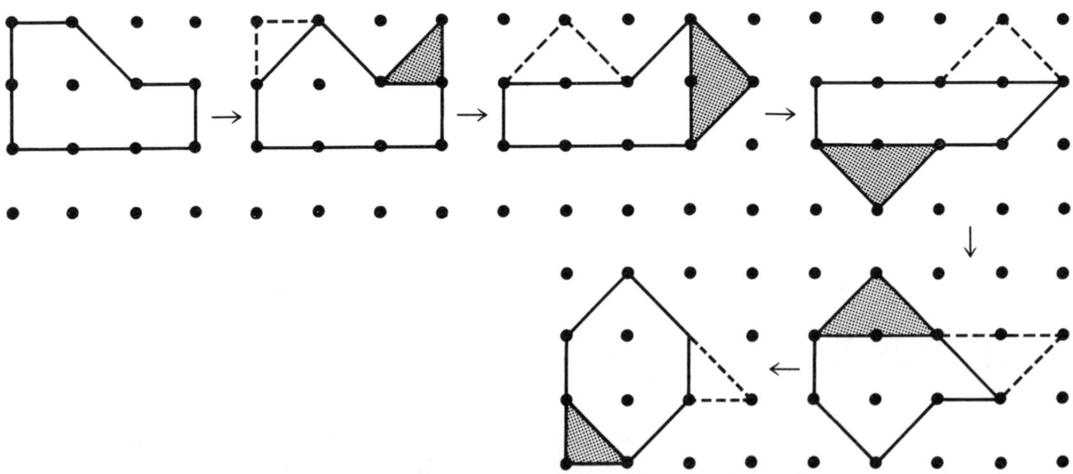

△ Try starting with a pentagon and keeping a pentagon shape.

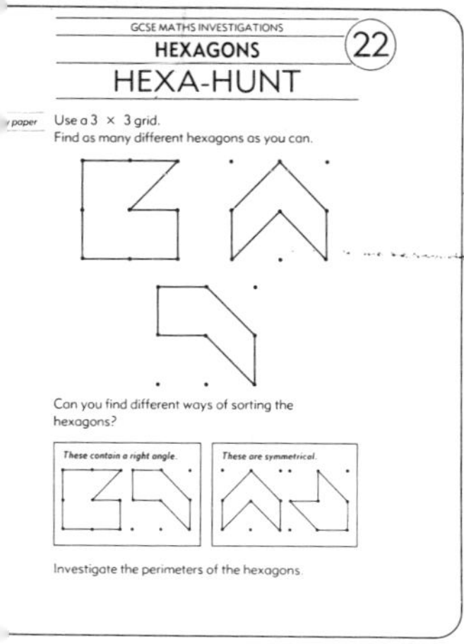
GCSE MATHS INVESTIGATIONS

HEXAGONS 22

HEXA-HUNT

...y paper

Use a 3 × 3 grid.
Find as many different hexagons as you can.

Can you find different ways of sorting the hexagons?

These contain a right angle.	*These are symmetrical.*

Investigate the perimeters of the hexagons.

GCSE MATHS INVESTIGATIONS

HEXAGONS

HEXAHUNT

22

Dotty paper

△ There are 22 possible hexagons:

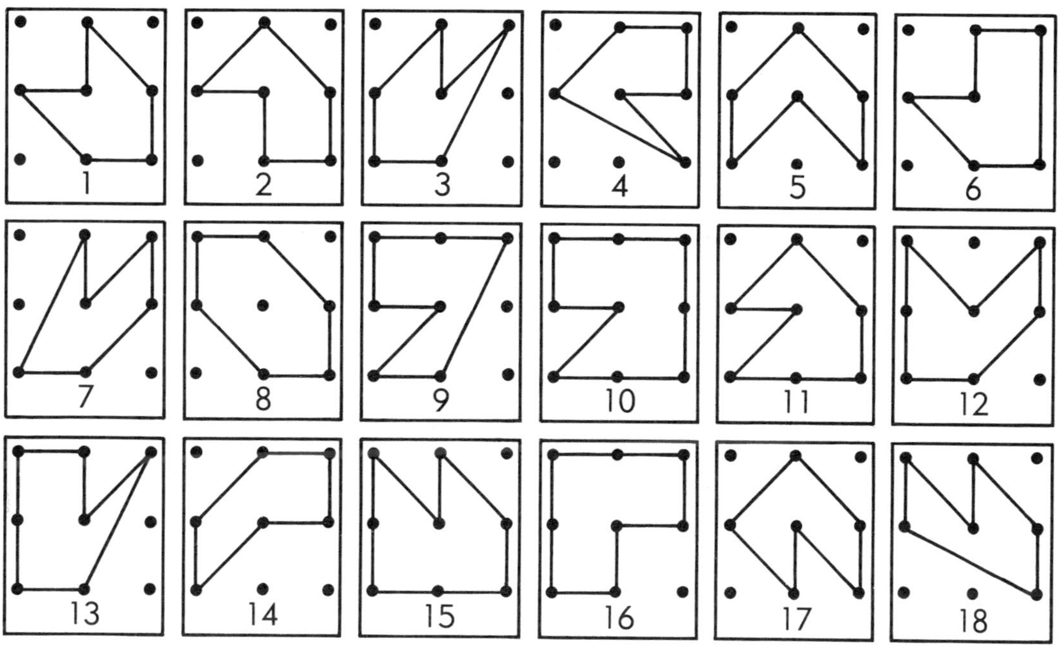

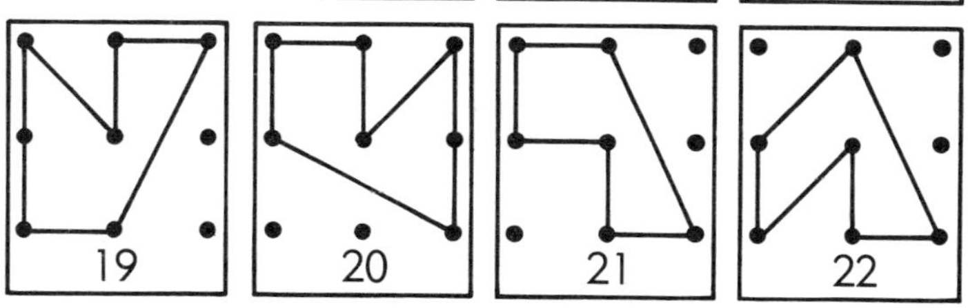

△ Possible classifications include:
line symmetry
1, 5, 8, 16
non-right angled
5, 7, 18
one right angle 1, 3, 5, 12, 22

△ Perimeters:
There are three unit lengths:

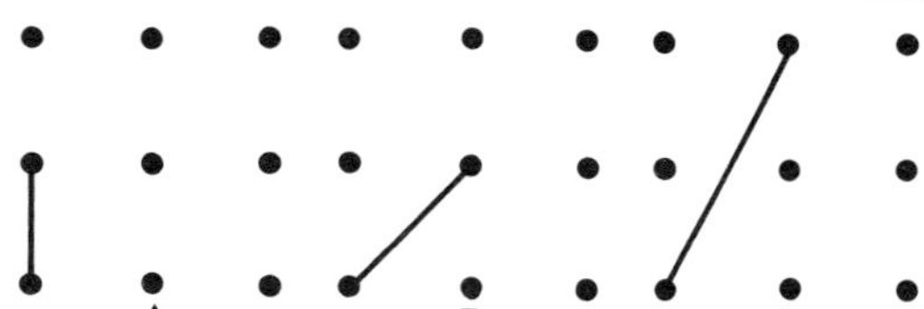

Hexagon 1 has a perimeter of $4A + 2B$.
Hexagon 2 has a perimeter of $4A + 2B$.
Hexagon 3 has a perimeter of $3A + 2B + C$.

△ Investigate the perimeter of the other hexagons.

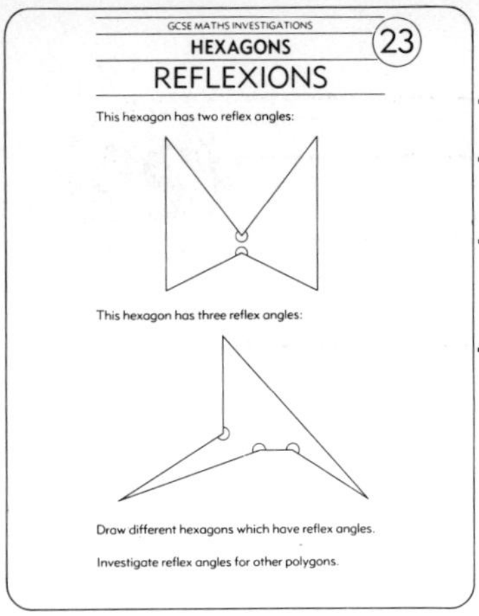

GCSE MATHS INVESTIGATIONS

HEXAGONS

REFLEXIONS

This hexagon has two reflex angles:

This hexagon has three reflex angles:

Draw different hexagons which have reflex angles.

Investigate reflex angles for other polygons.

23 HEXAGONS

REFLEXIONS

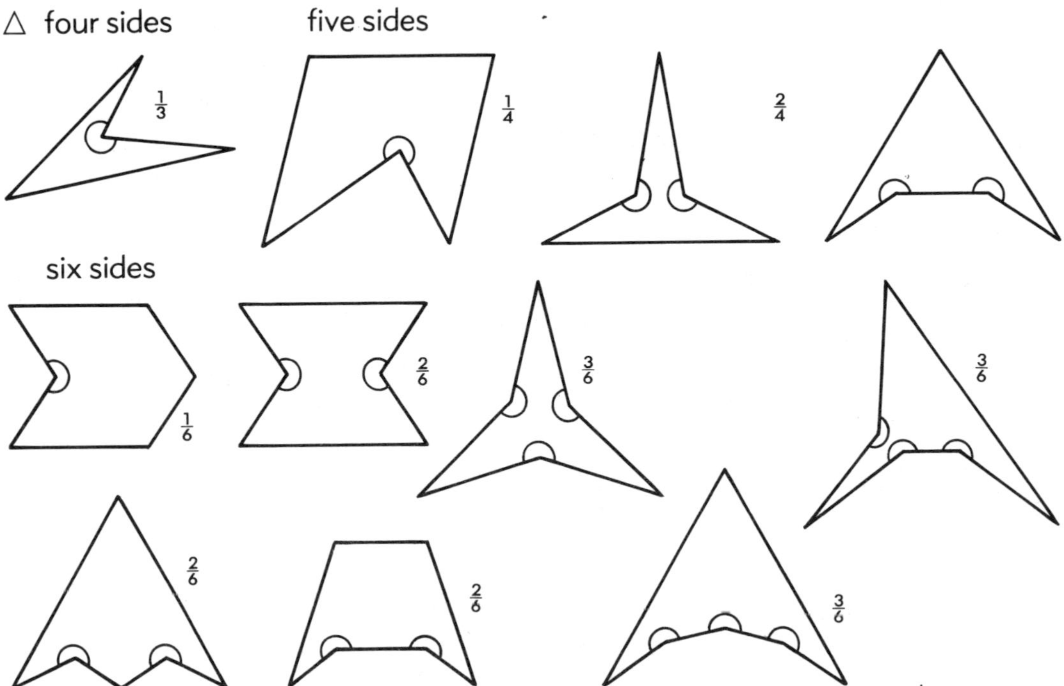

△ The sum of the interior angles of a hexagon is eight right angles. Therefore, the maximum number of reflex angles is three.

The maximum number of reflex angles on a '*n*'agon is $(n - 3)$.

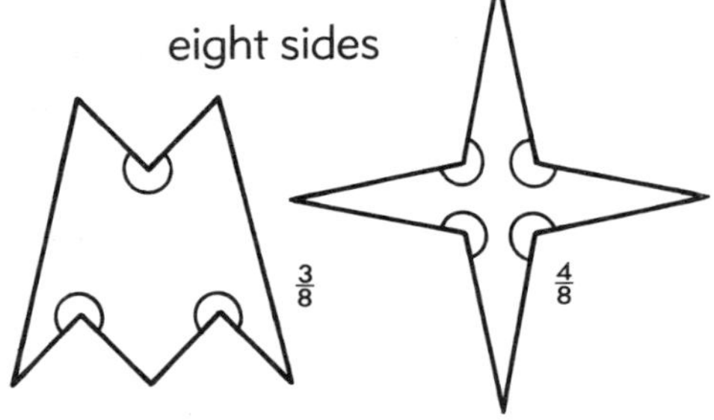

△ These are three types of hexagon containing two reflex angles. How can they be classified?

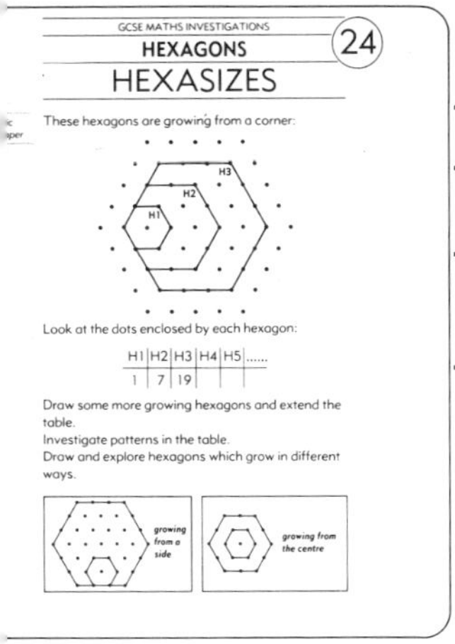

GCSE MATHS INVESTIGATIONS

HEXAGONS 24

HEXASIZES

These hexagons are growing from a corner:

Look at the dots enclosed by each hexagon:

H1	H2	H3	H4	H5	......
1	7	19			

Draw some more growing hexagons and extend the table.
Investigate patterns in the table.
Draw and explore hexagons which grow in different ways.

GCSE MATHS INVESTIGATIONS

HEXAGONS

HEXASIZES

24

Isometric dotty paper

△ Vertex-growing hexagons

H1	H2	H3	H4	H5	H6	H7	H8
1	7	19	37	61	91	127	169

H6 and H8 are not prime numbers. Which others are not?

△ Why are prime numbers so prominent?

The sequence of numbers is:
$(0 \times 6) + 1, (1 \times 6) + 1, (3 \times 6) + 1, (6 \times 6) + 1, (10 \times 6) + 1, \ldots$
The occurance of triangular numbers can be observed.

△ Consider the side-growing hexagons:

H1	H2	H3
1	19	61

When will the next non-prime number appear?

△ Try other growing polygons.

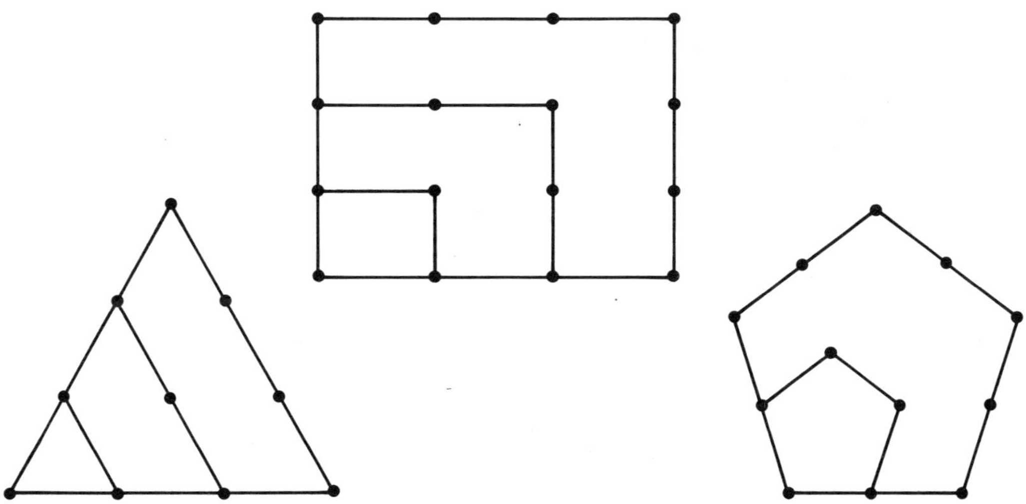

CARDS

	APPARATUS	ACTIVITY
25 Two-faced	Card	Arrangment of numbers to make totals
26 Prime rows	Number cards 1-9	Arrangement of numbers on a grid to sum to prime numbers
27 Nineteens	Number cards 1-9	Arrangment of numbers on a grid to make a constant total
28 Line-ups	Number cards 1-9	Arrangement of number to make equal totals
29 Double-edged	Card	Prime numbers
30 Primo	Number cards 1-9 Table of primes	Prime numbers
31 Card sums	Number cards 1-9	Addition sums
32 Paired totals	Number cards 0-20	Paring numbers summing to given totals

Some of these activities can be performed with pencil and paper, but the use of numbered cards is beneficial to most children. Small blank cards will be needed on which to write numerals, either on one or both sides. A copy master of numeral cards 0-20 is provided if required.

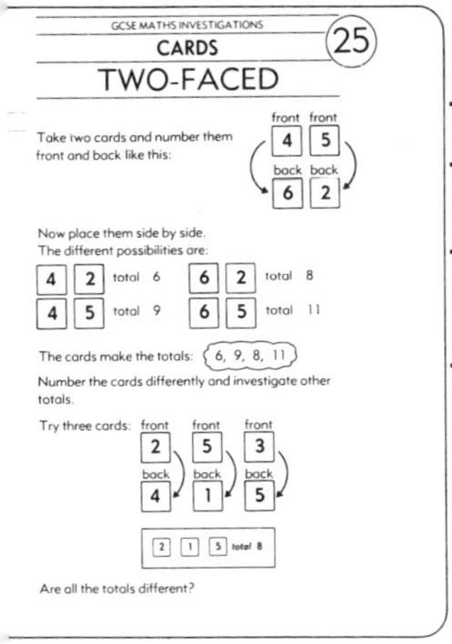
GCSE MATHS INVESTIGATIONS

CARDS

TWO-FACED

25

Take two cards and number them front and back like this:

front 4, back 6; front 5, back 2

Now place them side by side.
The different possibilities are:

4 2 total 6   6 2 total 8

4 5 total 9   6 5 total 11

The cards make the totals: 6, 9, 8, 11

Number the cards differently and investigate other totals.

Try three cards: front 2, back 4; front 5, back 1; front 3, back 5

2 1 5 total 8

Are all the totals different?

GCSE MATHS INVESTIGATIONS

CARDS

TWO FACED

25

Card

△ Three cards: Possible arrangements with 2/4, 5/1, 3/5 (front/back)

produces five consecutive even numbers from eight possible arrangements of cards: 6, 8, 10, 12, 14.

2 5 3 → 10	4 5 3 → 12
2 5 5 → 12	4 1 3 → 8
2 1 3 → 6	4 1 5 → 10
2 1 5 → 8	4 5 5 → 14

△ Is it possible to make the totals consecutive?

1/4, 2/3, 3/1 (front/back)

For these cards there are seven consecutive totals: 4, 5, 6, 7, 8, 9, 10.

1 2 3 → 6	4 2 3 → 9
1 2 1 → 4	4 2 1 → 7
1 3 3 → 7	4 3 3 → 10
1 3 1 → 5	4 3 1 → 8

△ A strategy is to consider two cards first:

e.g. 2/3, 3/1 (front/back)

The arrangements are:

2 1 → 3

3 1 → 4

2 3 → 5

3 3 → 6

So, including 1/5 (front/back) produces eight consecutive totals: 4, 5, 6, 7, 8, 9, 10, 11:

△ Which cards make these totals: 7, 8, 9, 10, 11, 12, 13, 14?

△ Can you make all totals even? odd?

E E O / E E O or O O O / O O O

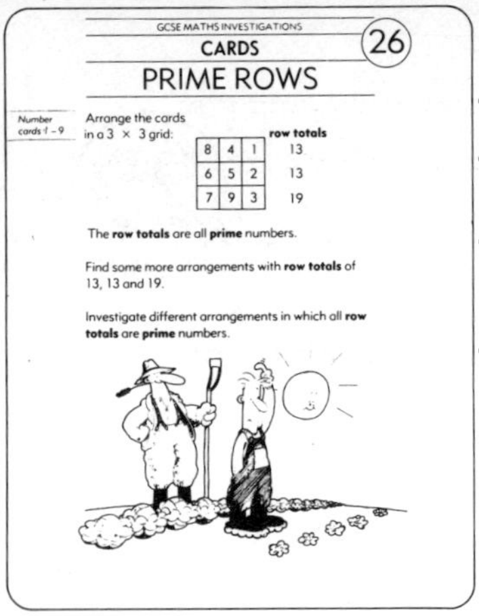
GCSE MATHS INVESTIGATIONS 26

CARDS

PRIME ROWS

Number cards 1-9

Arrange the cards in a 3 × 3 grid:

			row totals
8	4	1	13
6	5	2	13
7	9	3	19

The **row totals** are all **prime** numbers.

Find some more arrangements with **row totals** of 13, 13 and 19.

Investigate different arrangements in which all **row totals** are **prime** numbers.

GCSE MATHS INVESTIGATIONS

26

CARDS

PRIME ROWS

Number cards 1-9

△ Row totals: 13, 13 and 19
Some solutions:

8	4	1	13
6	5	2	13
7	9	3	19

2	8	3	13
7	5	1	13
9	6	4	19

6	4	3	13
7	5	1	13
9	8	2	19

4	7	8	19
9	3	1	13
2	5	6	13

△ Row totals: prime
The possible prime totals are: 7, 11, 13, 17, 19, 23
The three row totals must sum to 45.
Combinations of primes which sum to 45 are:

13 + 13 + 19   7 + 19 + 19
11 + 11 + 23   11 + 17 + 17

Some solutions include:

9	6	8	23
2	4	5	11
1	3	7	11

1	2	4	7
3	7	9	19
5	6	8	19

1	3	7	11
4	5	8	17
2	6	9	17

△ Is it possible to make row totals <u>and</u> column totals prime?

6	4	9	19
5	7	1	13
8	2	3	13
19	13	13	

8	6	5	19
9	3	1	13
2	4	7	13
19	13	13	

△ Is it possible to include the diagonals also?

△ Change the numbers on the cards. Change the size of the grid.

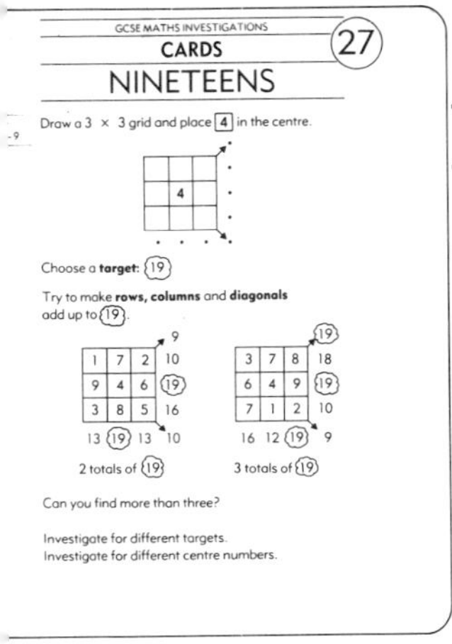
GCSE MATHS INVESTIGATIONS
CARDS
NINETEENS
27

Draw a 3 × 3 grid and place 4 in the centre.

Choose a **target**: 19

Try to make **rows, columns** and **diagonals** add up to 19.

1	7	2	10
9	4	6	19
3	8	5	16
13	19	13	10

(diagonal: 9)

2 totals of 19

3	7	8	18
6	4	9	19
7	1	2	10
16	12	19	9

(diagonal: 19)

3 totals of 19

Can you find more than three?

Investigate for different targets.
Investigate for different centre numbers.

GCSE MATHS INVESTIGATIONS

CARDS

NINETEENS

27

Number cards 1-9

Some solutions include:

△ centre 4, target 19 — 5 totals

7	1	6	14
3	4	5	12
9	2	8	19
19	7	19	19

(diagonal ↗: 19)

△ centre 4, target 18 — 5 totals

6	7	5	18
3	4	2	9
9	1	8	18
18	12	15	18

(diagonal ↗: 18)

△ centre 4, target 17 — 4 totals

6	1	5	12
3	4	9	16
8	2	7	17
17	7	21	17

(diagonal ↗: 17)

△ centre 4, target 15 — 6 totals

6	9	3	18
1	4	7	12
8	2	5	15
15	15	15	15

(diagonal ↗: 15)

△ Results can be tabulated:

	Total								
Centre number			15	16	17	18	19		
4			6		4	5	5		

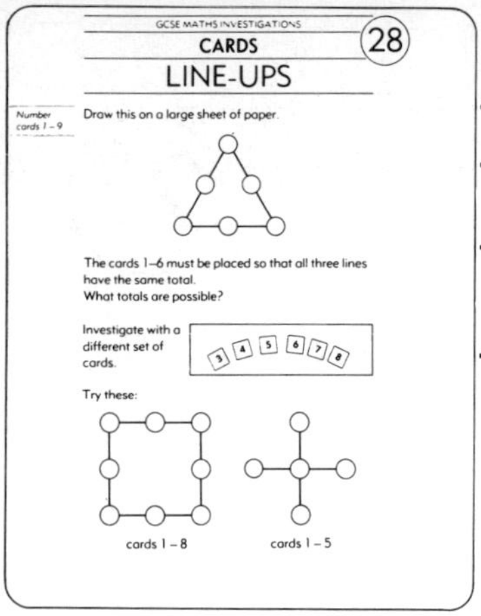

GCSE MATHS INVESTIGATIONS

CARDS

28

LINE-UPS

Number cards 1 – 9

Draw this on a large sheet of paper.

The cards 1–6 must be placed so that all three lines have the same total.
What totals are possible?

Investigate with a different set of cards. 3 4 5 6 7 8

Try these:

cards 1 – 8 cards 1 – 5

CARDS

LINE-UPS

Number cards 1-9

△ Cards 1-6

total 9	total 10	total 11	total 12
1	1	2	4
6 5	6 4	3 5	3 2
2 4 3	3 2 5	6 1 4	5 1 6

△ With cards 2-7, totals are 12, 13, 14, 15.

Cards	Totals
1 – 6	9, 10, 11, 12
2 – 7	12, 13, 14, 15
3 – 8	15, 16, 17, 18
⋮	⋮ ⋮ ⋮ ⋮
9 – 14	33, 34, 35, 36

△ Solutions:

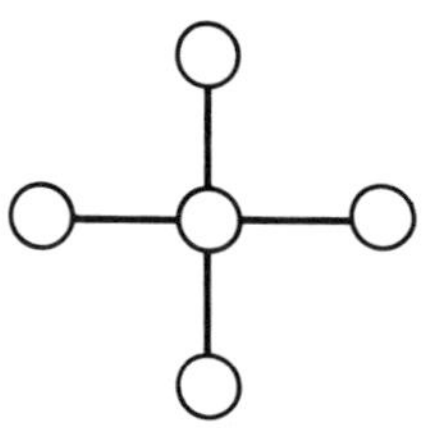

Cards 1 – 5

total 8	total 9	total 10
2	1	1
3 1 4	2 3 4	2 5 3
5	5	4

△ Cards 1 – 8 One approach is to list all possibilities that sum to 13:

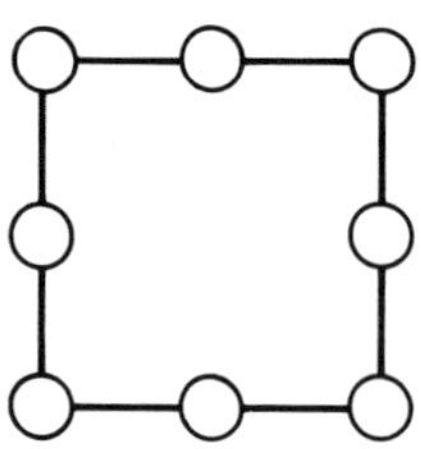

i.e. 1 – 8 – 4 2 – 7 – 4
1 – 7 – 5 2 – 6 – 5
2 – 8 – 3 3 – 6 – 4

1 7 5
4 6
8 3 2

total 13

Totals 14 and 15 are also possible.

GCSE MATHS INVESTIGATIONS

CARDS

29

DOUBLE-EDGED

Take three cards and number them front and back like this:

Arrange **two** cards to make a **two-digit** number.

e.g. 2 1

How many different **two-digit** numbers can be made?

Try with a different set of three cards.

Try numbering three cards to make as many **two-digit prime** numbers as you can.

Investigate other types of numbers.

square numbers multiples of 7

GCSE MATHS INVESTIGATIONS

CARDS

DOUBLE EDGED

29

Card

△ 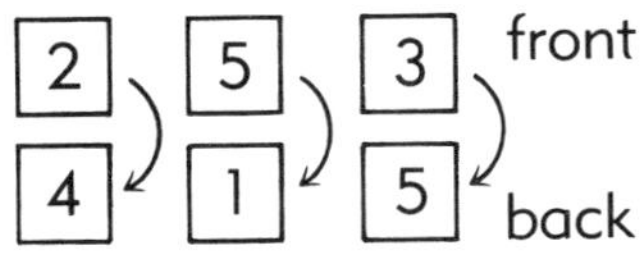

19 different two-digit numbers are possible:

12	21	31	41	51
13	23	32	43	52
14	25	34	45	53
15		35		54
				55

△ 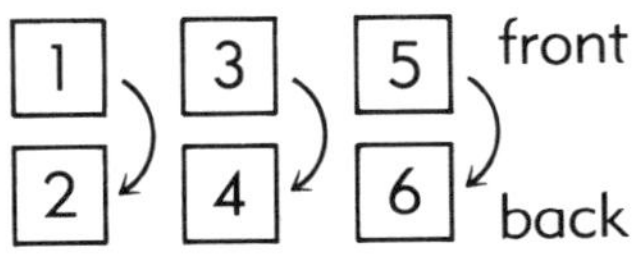

This arrangement produces the maximum 24 two-digit numbers:

13	23	31	41	51	61
14	24	32	42	52	62
15	25	35	45	53	63
16	26	36	46	54	64

△ What is the maximum if only five **different** digits are used?

△ The two-digit prime numbers are:

11		31	41		61	71		91
13			43	53		73	83	
17		37						97
19	29		47	59	67	79	89	

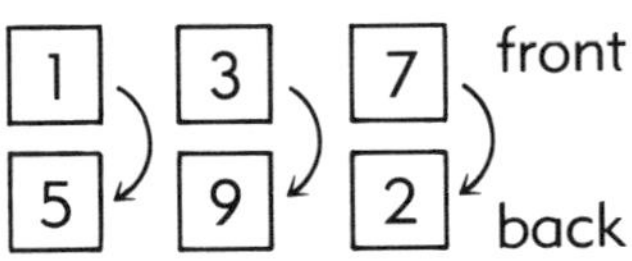

This arrangement produces 14 different prime numbers:

13	23	31	53	71	91
17	29	37	59	73	97
19				79	

Is it possible to find more than 14?

△ 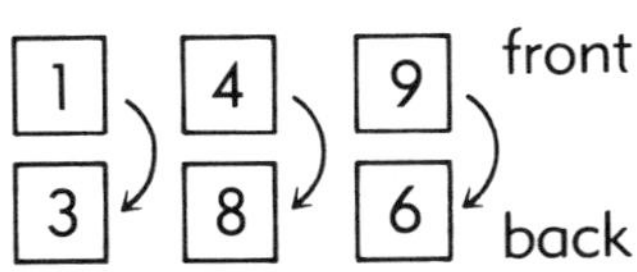

This arrangement produces the following two-digit square numbers: 16, 36, 49, 64, 81

Can this be improved upon?

GCSE MATHS INVESTIGATIONS

CARDS 30

PRIMO

Number cards 1-9

Table of primes

Choose three cards: [1] [3] [4]

The following **prime numbers** can be made:

[3] [4][3]
[1][3] [3][1]
[4][1] [4][3][1]

i.e. (6) altogether

Investigate for other sets of three cards.

Choose four cards.

Make square numbers.

GCSE MATHS INVESTIGATIONS

CARDS (30)

PRIMO

Number cards 1-9

Table of primes

△ Use the table of primes.

△ One strategy is to state all possible single-digit, two-digit and three-digit numbers using the three cards, and then make a search for primes. Another strategy is to start by looking at a list of primes.

△ [1] [2] [3] : Possible numbers are:

1	12	123
2 √	13 √	132
3 √	21	213
	31 √	231
	23 √	312
	32	321

So,

[1] [2] [3] → 5 primes

△ [5] [3] [9] : Possible numbers are:

3 √	35	359 √
5 √	39	395
9	53 √	539
	59 √	593
	93	935
	95	953 √

[5] [3] [9] → 6 primes

△ Other solutions include:

[1] [7] [9] → 10 primes

1	17 √	179 √
7 √	19 √	197 √
9	71 √	719 √
	79 √	791
	91	917
	97 √	971 √

[1] [3] [7] → 11 primes

1	13 √	137 √
3 √	17 √	173 √
7 √	31 √	317 √
	37 √	371
	71 √	713
	73 √	731

△ What is the maximum?

△ What is the maximum if (a) one card must be even?
(b) two cards must be even?

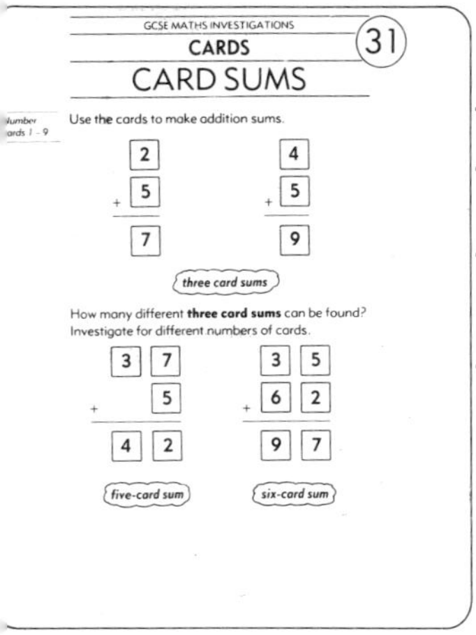
GCSE MATHS INVESTIGATIONS
CARDS 31
CARD SUMS
Number cards 1-9
Use the cards to make addition sums.
$$\begin{array}{r} 2 \\ +\ 5 \\ \hline 7 \end{array} \qquad \begin{array}{r} 4 \\ +\ 5 \\ \hline 9 \end{array}$$
three card sums
How many different **three card sums** can be found?
Investigate for different numbers of cards.
$$\begin{array}{r} 37 \\ +\ 5 \\ \hline 42 \end{array} \qquad \begin{array}{r} 35 \\ +\ 62 \\ \hline 97 \end{array}$$
five-card sum six-card sum

GCSE MATHS INVESTIGATIONS

CARDS

CARD SUMS

31

Number cards 1-9

△ three-card solutions – 16 altogether

$$\begin{array}{cccccccccccccccc} 1 & 1 & 1 & 1 & 1 & 1 & 1 & 2 & 2 & 2 & 2 & 2 & 3 & 3 & 3 & 4 \\ 2 & 3 & 4 & 5 & 6 & 7 & 8 & 3 & 4 & 5 & 6 & 7 & 4 & 5 & 6 & 5 \\ \hline 3 & 4 & 5 & 6 & 7 & 8 & 9 & 5 & 6 & 7 & 8 & 9 & 7 & 8 & 9 & 9 \end{array}$$

Which answer appears most often? Which answer appears least often?
Which answers are impossible?
Which card has been used most times?

△ four-card solutions – 12 altogether.

$$\begin{array}{cccccccccccc} 3 & 4 & 5 & 6 & 7 & 8 & 4 & 5 & 6 & 7 & 5 & 6 \\ 9 & 9 & 9 & 9 & 9 & 9 & 8 & 8 & 8 & 8 & 7 & 7 \\ \hline 12 & 13 & 14 & 15 & 16 & 17 & 12 & 13 & 14 & 15 & 12 & 13 \end{array}$$

△ Other solutions include:

$$\begin{array}{r} 36 \\ 9 \\ \hline 45 \end{array} \qquad \begin{array}{r} 23 \\ 45 \\ \hline 68 \end{array} \qquad \begin{array}{r} 73 \\ 69 \\ \hline 142 \end{array} \qquad \begin{array}{r} 854 \\ 67 \\ \hline 921 \end{array} \qquad \begin{array}{r} 234 \\ 657 \\ \hline 891 \end{array}$$

5 cards 6 cards 7 cards 8 cards 9 cards

How many different solutions can be found for each type?

△ Which is the smallest and which is the largest possible answer for different numbers of cards?

△ Extend to subtraction and multiplication sums.

△ Explore sums using consecutive cards:

$1 + 2 = 3$	3 card
$46 + 7 = 53$	5 card
$35 + 6 + 7 = 48$	6 card

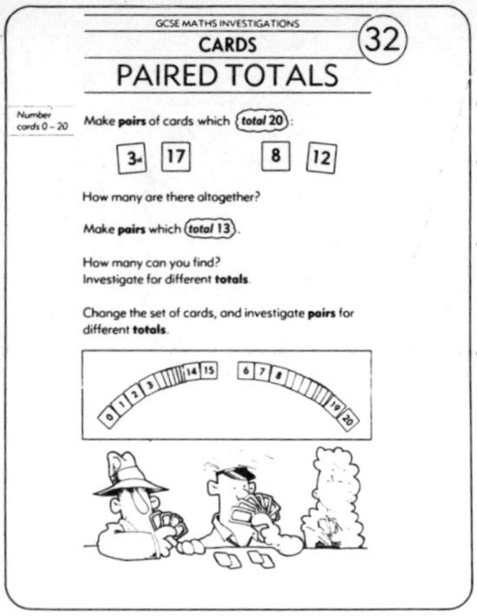

GCSE MATHS INVESTIGATIONS

CARDS

PAIRED TOTALS

32

Number cards 0 – 20

Make **pairs** of cards which (*total* 20):

3 17   8 12

How many are there altogether?

Make **pairs** which (*total* 13).

How many can you find?
Investigate for different **totals**.

Change the set of cards, and investigate **pairs** for different **totals**.

GCSE MATHS INVESTIGATIONS

CARDS

PAIRED TOTALS

32

Set of cards 0-20

△ Total 20 produces 10 pairs.
Total 13 produces 7 pairs.
(0, 13), (1, 12), (2, 11), (3, 10), (4, 9), (5, 8), (6, 7)

△ The results can be tabulated:

Total	1/2	3/4	5/6	7/8	9/10	11/12	13/14	15/16	17/18	19/20
Pairs	1	2	3	4	5	6	7	8	9	10

So, for total n: n even $\rightarrow \frac{n}{2}$ pairs

n odd $\rightarrow \frac{n+1}{2}$ pairs

△ Consider totals greater than 20:
total 30: (10, 20), (11, 19), (12, 18), (13, 17), (14, 16)

Total	21	22/23	24/25	26/27	28/29	30/31	32/33	34/35	36/37	38/39
Pairs	10	9	8	7	6	5	4	3	2	1

So for total n: n even $\rightarrow 20 - \frac{n}{2}$ pairs

n odd $\rightarrow 20 - \left(\frac{n-1}{2}\right)$ pairs

△ If the set of cards are reduced to 0-15, then:
for $n \leqslant 15$ results are the same as for 0-20 cards.
for $n > 15$: n even $\rightarrow 15 - \frac{n}{2}$ pairs

n odd $\rightarrow 15 - \left(\frac{n-1}{2}\right)$ pairs

△ Investigate pairs for different sets of cards:
6-20
10-20   5-15

△ Investigate PAIRS with fixed DIFFERENCES instead of TOTALS:
(0,7), (1,8), (2,9), (3,10), (4,11), (5,12), (6,13) have a difference of 7.

TRIANGLES

	APPARATUS	ACTIVITY
33 Sticks	Matches	Triangles with constant perimeters
34 Equilaterals	Isometric dotty paper	Searching for different sized equilateral triangles
35 Appointments	Tracing paper	Different shapes from common vertices
36 Relaps		Maximising the number of triangles produced from a given number of straight lines
37 Chops	Isometric paper Scissors	Removing triangles to make polygons
38 Trifits	Isometric paper Scissors	Joining equilateral triangles to make hexagons. Tesellation
39 Joints	Isosceles right-angled triangles	Joining isosceles right-angled triangles
40 Models	Card Scissors Glue	Making 3-D models from equilateral triangles

The theme of **triangles** provides a starting point for activities on a variety of geometrical ideas both two and three dimensional.

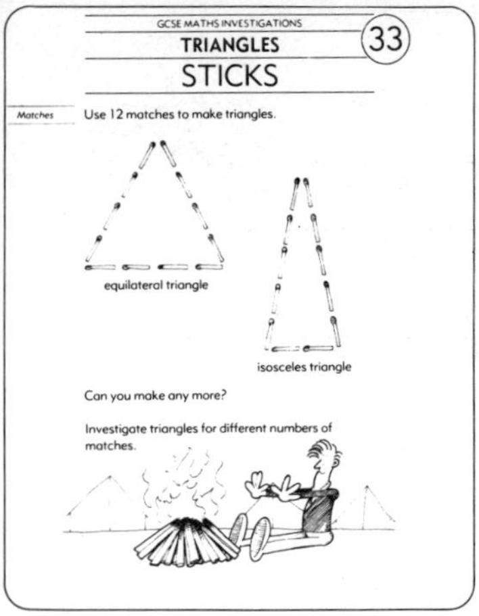
GCSE MATHS INVESTIGATIONS

TRIANGLES 33

STICKS

Matches

Use 12 matches to make triangles.

equilateral triangle

isosceles triangle

Can you make any more?

Investigate triangles for different numbers of matches.

GCSE MATHS INVESTIGATIONS

TRIANGLES 33

STICKS

Matchsticks

△ One approach is to consider the set of triples which sum to 12, and then search for those which will form triangles (i.e. the longest side is less than the sum of the other two).

12 matches (1, 1, 10) (1, 2, 9,) (1, 3, 8,) (1, 4, 7,) (1, 5, 6,)
(2, 2, 8) (2, 3, 7,) (2, 4, 9,) (2, 5, 5)
(3, 3, 6) (3, 4, 5)
(4, 4, 4)

△ Some solutions include:

3 matches: (1, 1, 1)

4 matches: none possible

5 matches: (1, 2, 2)

6 matches: (2, 2, 2)

7 matches: (1, 3, 3) (2, 2, 3)

8 matches: (2, 3, 3)

9 matches: (1, 4, 4) (2, 3, 4) (3, 3, 3)

10 matches: (2, 4, 4) (3, 3, 4)

11 matches: (2, 4, 5) (3, 4, 4)

12 matches: (2, 5, 5) (3, 4, 5) (4, 4, 4)

13 matches: (1, 6, 6) (2, 5, 6) (3, 5, 5) (3, 4, 6) (4, 4, 5)

14 matches: (2, 6, 6) (3, 5, 6) (4, 4, 6) (4, 5, 5)

15 matches: (1, 7, 7) (2, 6, 7) (3, 5, 7) (3, 6, 6) (4, 4, 7) (4, 5, 6) (5, 5, 5)

△ Is it possible to predict the number of solutions for a given number of matches?
△ Investigate types of quadrilaterals made from 8 matches, 9 matches, ...
△ Which arrangements produce: equilateral triangles?
right-angled triangles?
obtuse-angled triangles?
isosceles triangles?

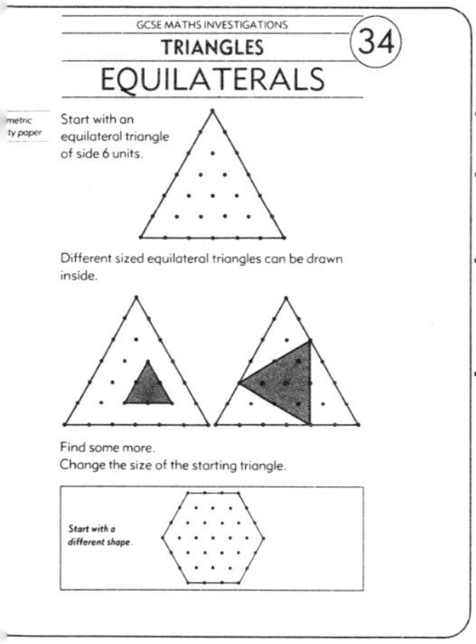
GCSE MATHS INVESTIGATIONS

TRIANGLES (34)

EQUILATERALS

Start with an equilateral triangle of side 6 units.

Different sized equilateral triangles can be drawn inside.

Find some more.
Change the size of the starting triangle.

Start with a different shape.

GCSE MATHS INVESTIGATIONS

TRIANGLES (34)

EQUILATERALS

Isometric dotty paper

△ Consider the different types of triangles:

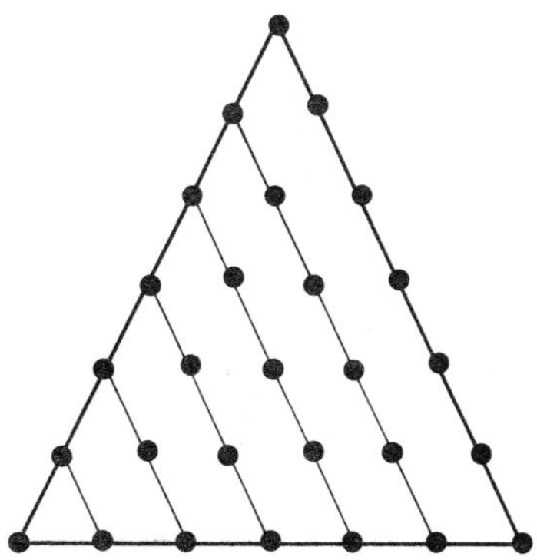
triangles with sides parallel to the original

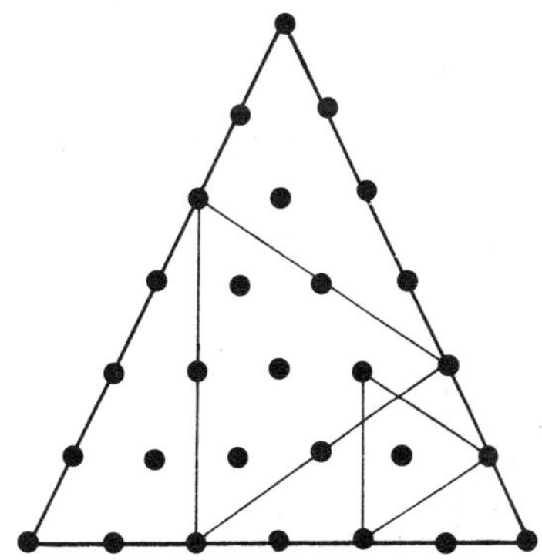
similar skew triangles

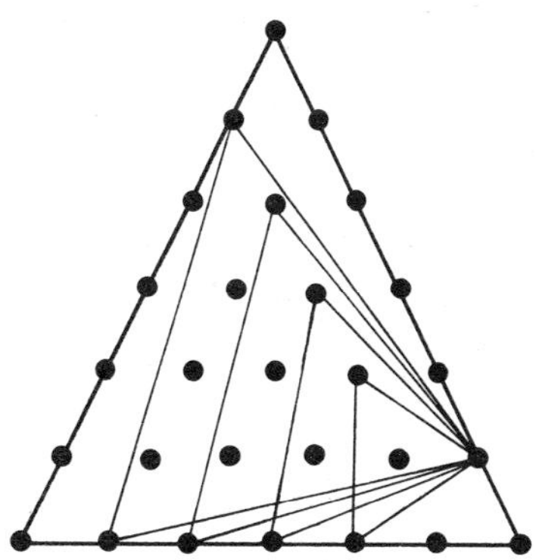
skew triangles with no perimeter dots

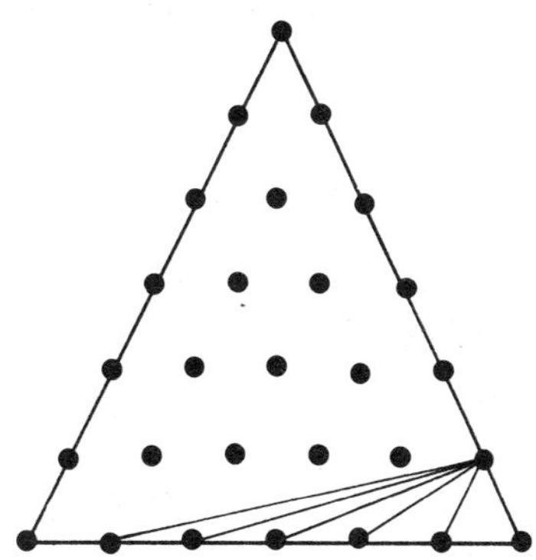
Consider the possible side lengths: a, $\sqrt{3}a$, $\sqrt{7}a$, $\sqrt{13}a$; etc.

△ Extend to searching for shapes other than triangles: parallelograms, hexagons.

△ Use a different starting shape, such as a rhombus.

△ Consider shapes using square dotty paper.

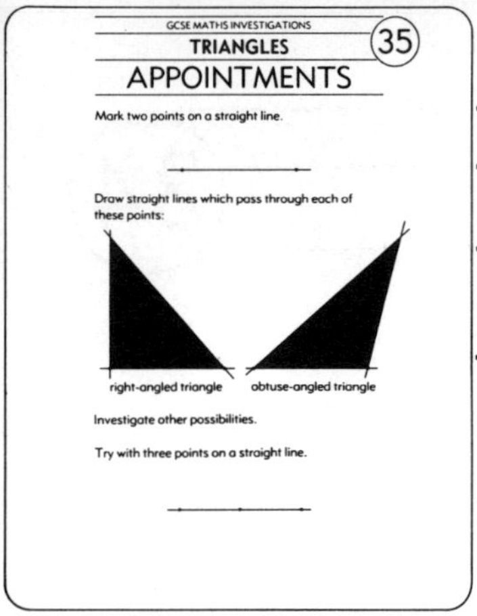

GCSE MATHS INVESTIGATIONS
TRIANGLES 35
APPOINTMENTS

Mark two points on a straight line.

Draw straight lines which pass through each of these points:

right-angled triangle obtuse-angled triangle

Investigate other possibilities.

Try with three points on a straight line.

GCSE MATHS INVESTIGATIONS

TRIANGLES

APPOINTMENTS

35

Tracing paper

△ A useful aid is straight lines drawn on acetate sheets or tracing paper.

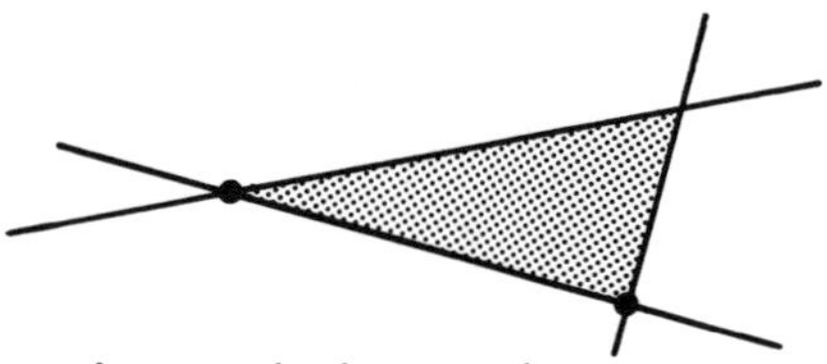

right-angled triangle

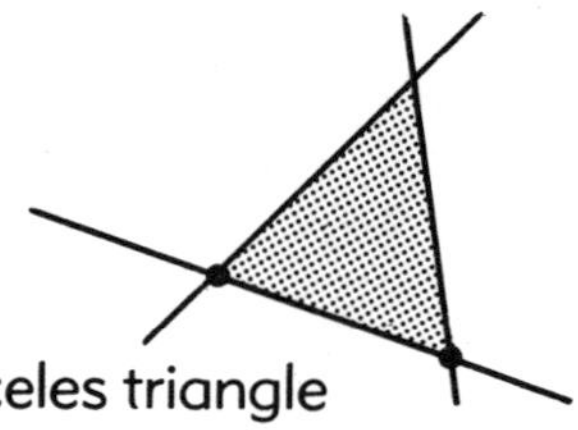

isosceles triangle

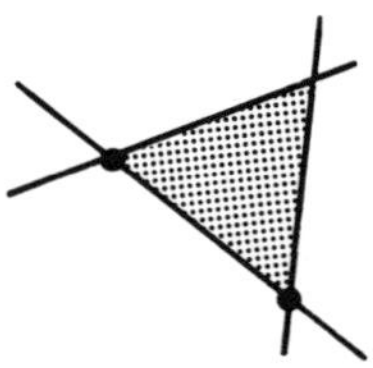

equilateral triangle

obtuse-angled triangle

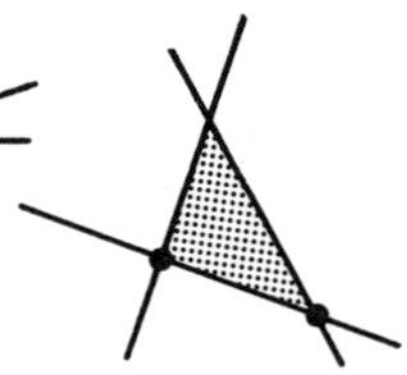

isosceles right-angled triangle

△ Three points: One approach is to keep two lines fixed and experiment with the third.

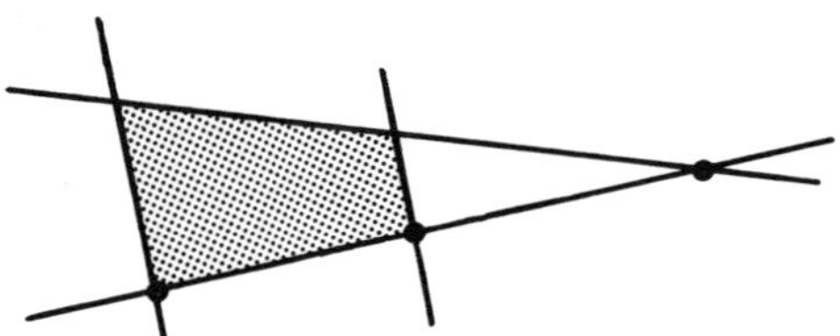

trapezium

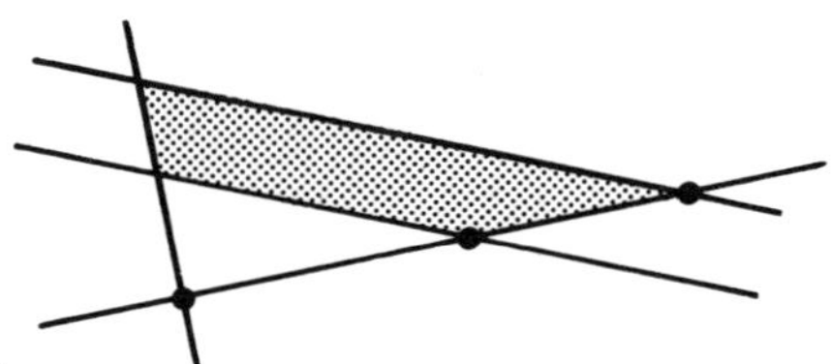

trapezium

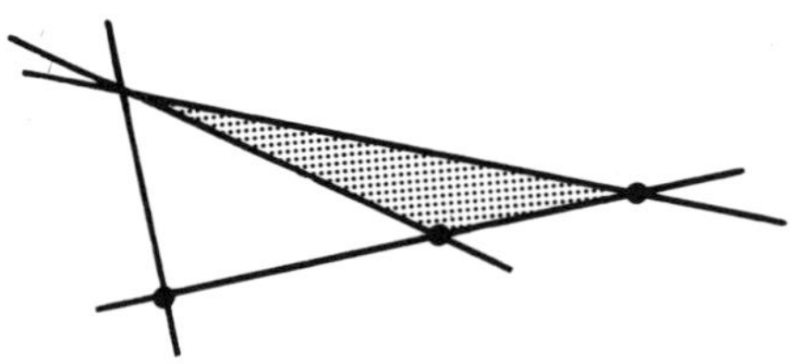

obtuse-angled triangle

△ Try points not on a straight line, such as on a circle.

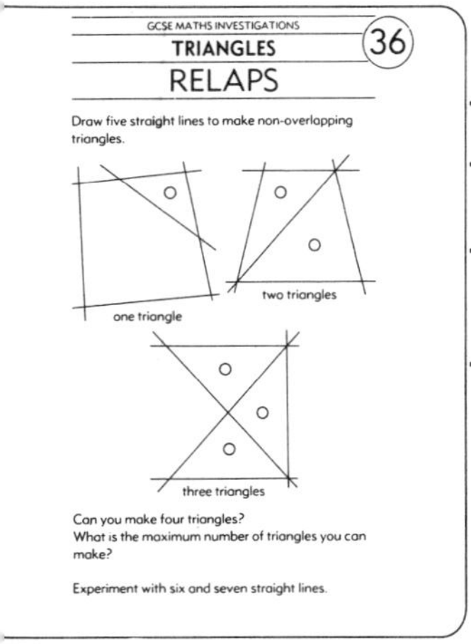
GCSE MATHS INVESTIGATIONS

TRIANGLES 36

RELAPS

Draw five straight lines to make non-overlapping triangles.

one triangle

two triangles

three triangles

Can you make four triangles?
What is the maximum number of triangles you can make?

Experiment with six and seven straight lines.

GCSE MATHS INVESTIGATIONS

TRIANGLES

RELAPS

36

Tracing paper

- △ A useful aid is straight lines drawn on acetate sheets or tracing paper.
- △ With five lines:

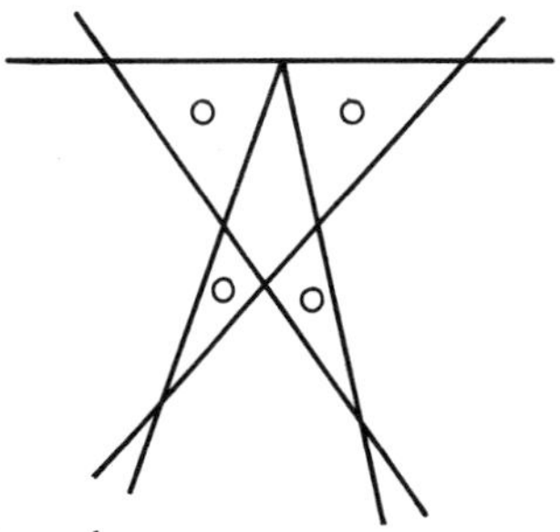

4 triangles

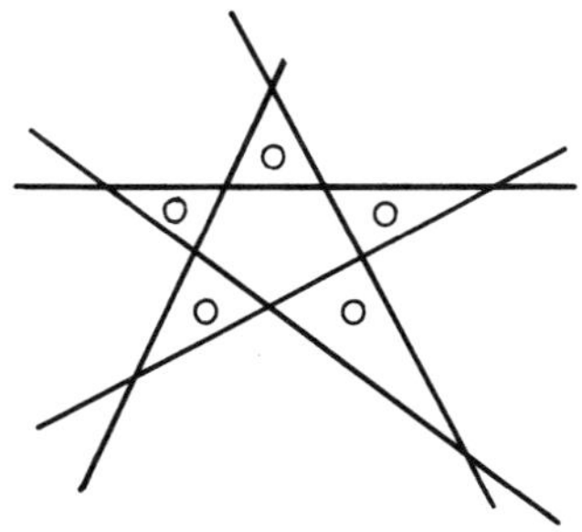

5 triangles

Is five triangles the maximum?

- △ With six lines:

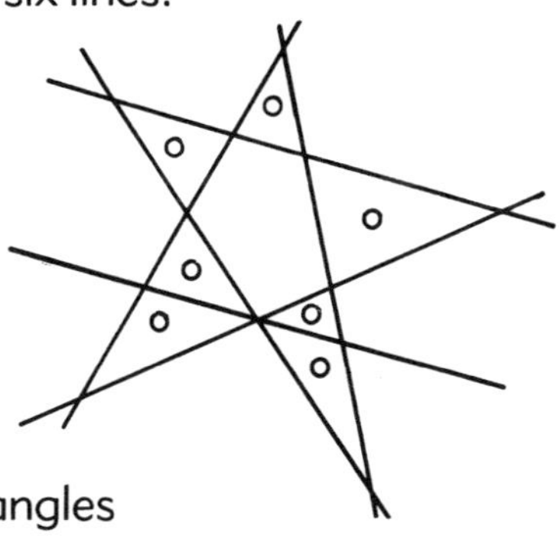

7 triangles

With seven lines:

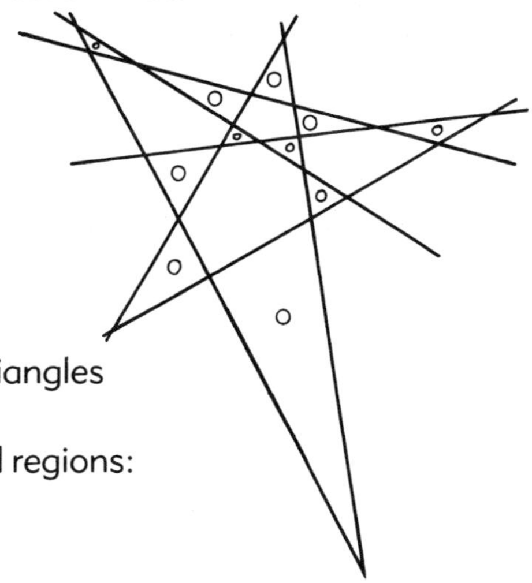

11 triangles

- △ Extend to consideration of other enclosed regions: six lines

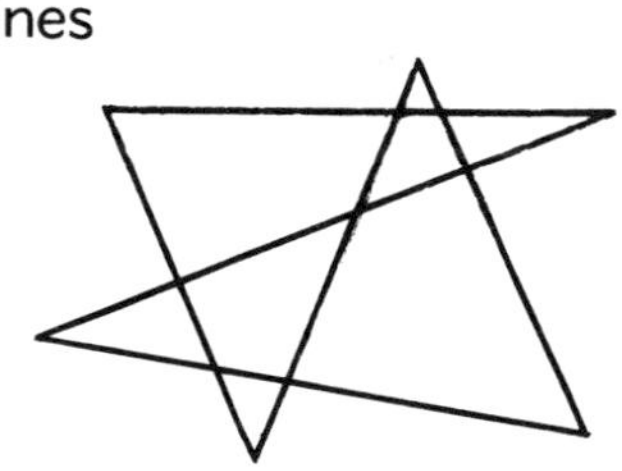

eight regions: four triangles and four quadrilaterals: $(3^4 + 4^4)$

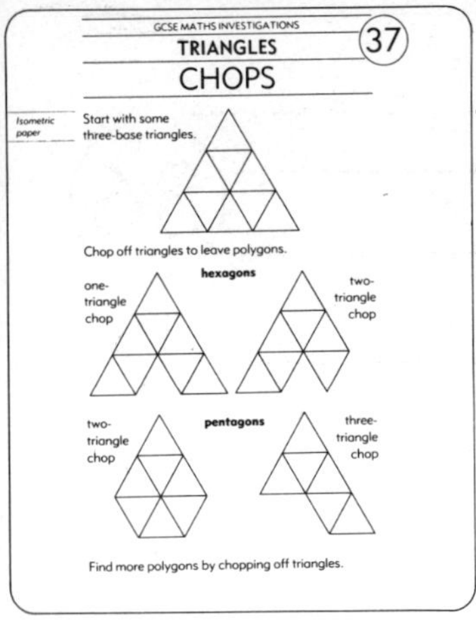

GCSE MATHS INVESTIGATIONS

TRIANGLES

CHOPS

37

Isometric paper
Scissors

△ Consider the polygons made by chopping two triangles:

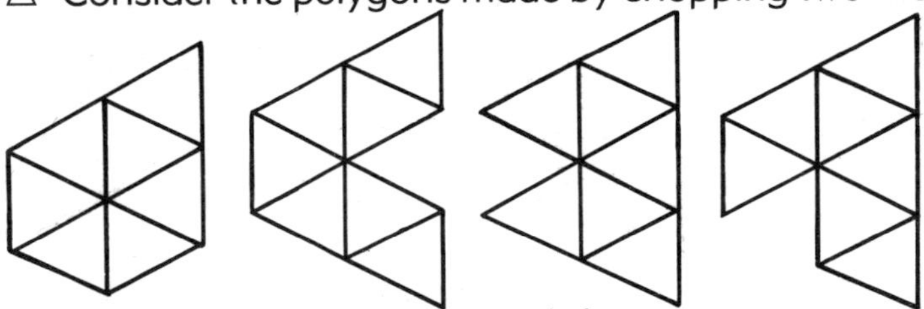

There are three symmetrical shapes.
Are these the only possibilities?

△ Polygons made by chopping three triangles:

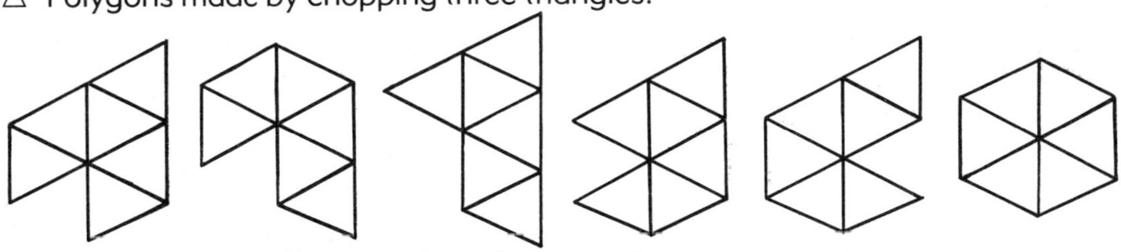

△ Different "chops" can produce the same shape:

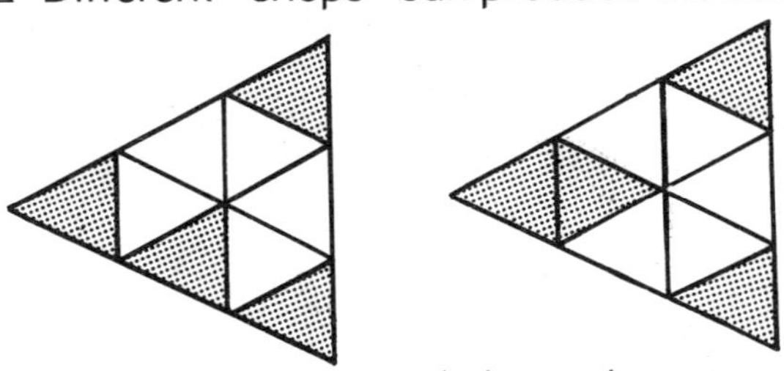

△ What can be noticed about chopping six triangles?

△ Consider polygons made by chopping triangles from four-base triangles:

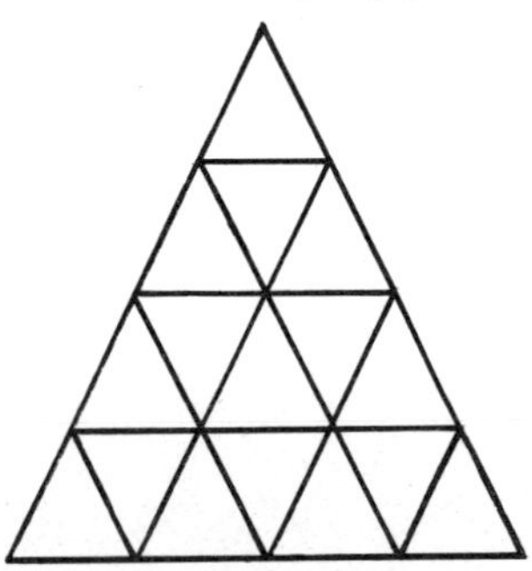

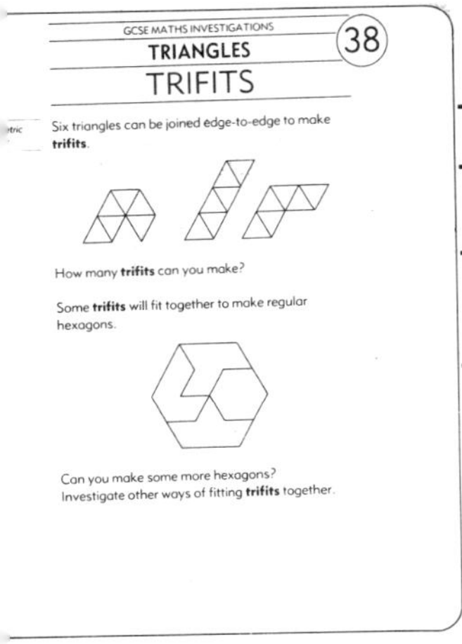
GCSE MATHS INVESTIGATIONS

TRIANGLES (38)

TRIFITS

Six triangles can be joined edge-to-edge to make **trifits**.

How many **trifits** can you make?

Some **trifits** will fit together to make regular hexagons.

Can you make some more hexagons?
Investigate other ways of fitting **trifits** together.

GCSE MATHS INVESTIGATIONS

TRIANGLES

TRIFITS

(38)

Isometric paper

Scissors

△ There are 12 possible **trifits**:

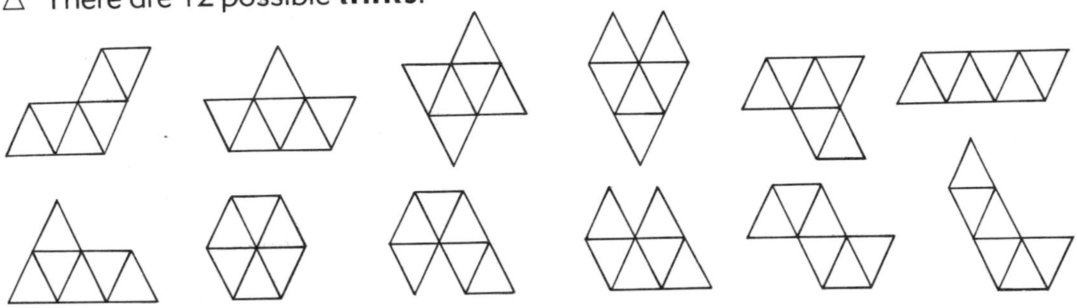

△ Regular hexagons can be made:

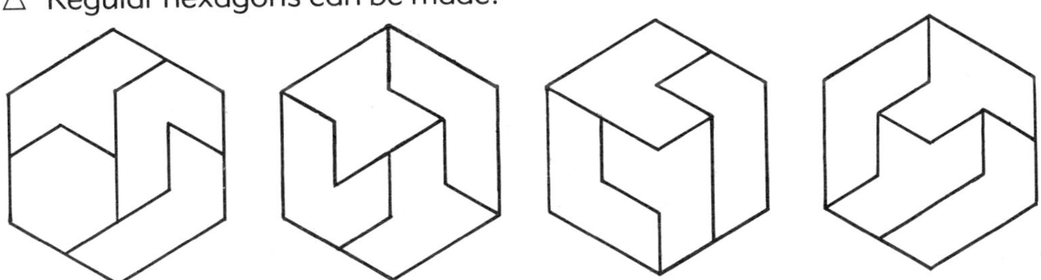

4 trifit hexagons

9 trifit hexagons

△ Which **trifits** tessellate?

△ Investigate perimeters of **trifits**.

△ All 12 trifits can be fitted together to make a rhombus or a "disappointed" equilateral triangle.

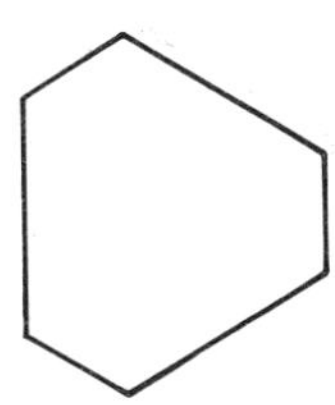

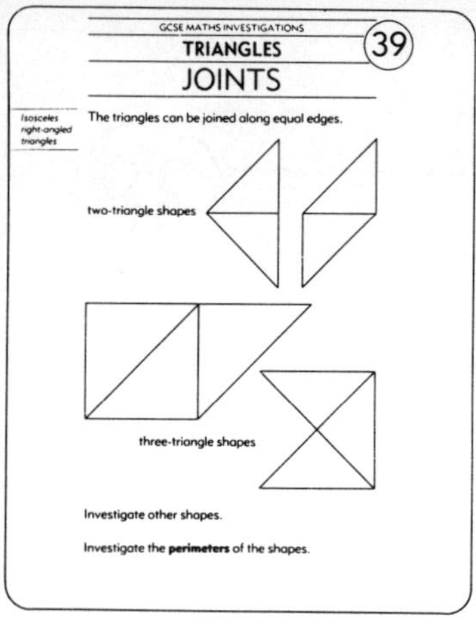
GCSE MATHS INVESTIGATIONS

TRIANGLES (39)

JOINTS

Isosceles right-angled triangles

The triangles can be joined along equal edges.

two-triangle shapes

three-triangle shapes

Investigate other shapes.

Investigate the **perimeters** of the shapes.

GCSE MATHS INVESTIGATIONS

TRIANGLES (39)

JOINTS

Isoceles right-angled triangles

△ Possible shapes include:

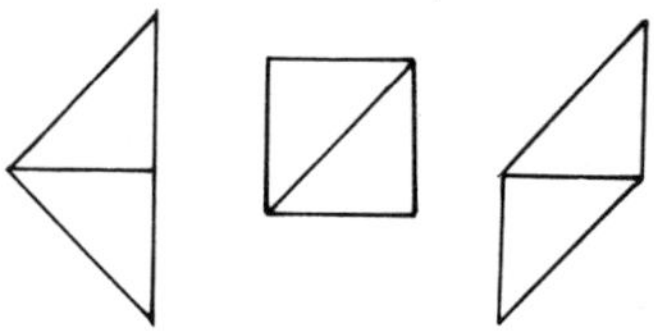

two triangles

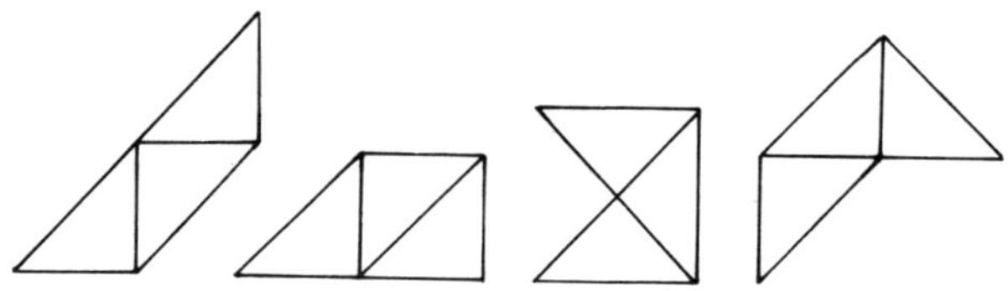

three triangles

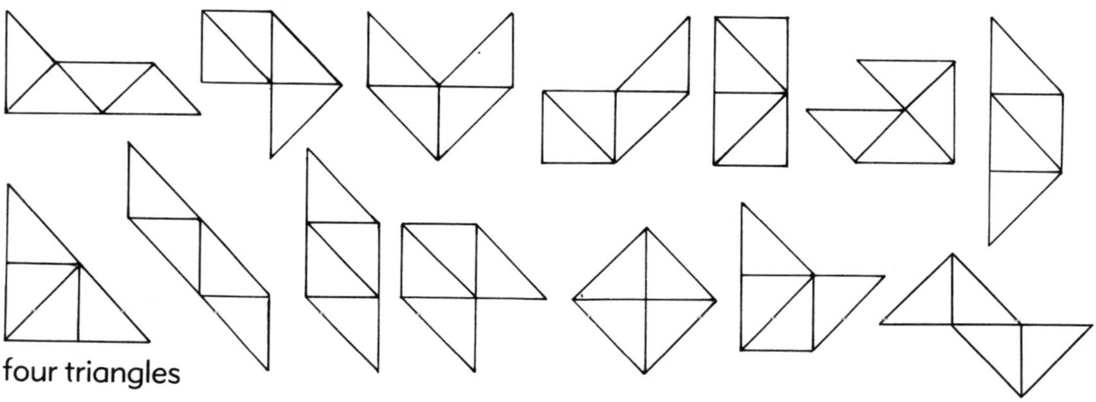

four triangles

△ Two lengths of side exist for each triangle. So, for example:

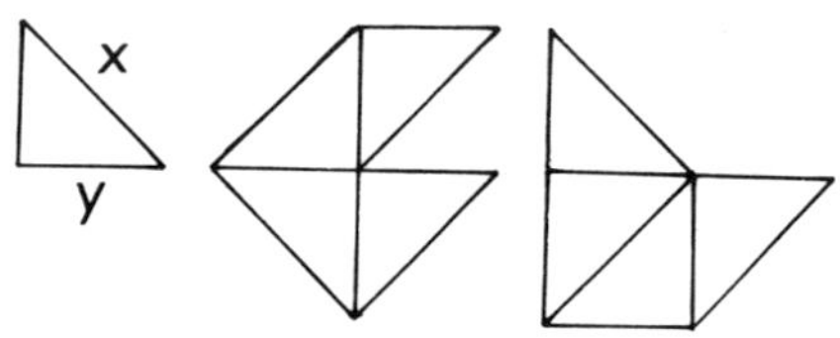

perimeter $2x + 4y$ perimeter $4x + 2y$

△

Number of triangles	*Number of different shapes*
1	1
2	3
3	4
4	14
5	30
6	107

No obvious pattern emerges.

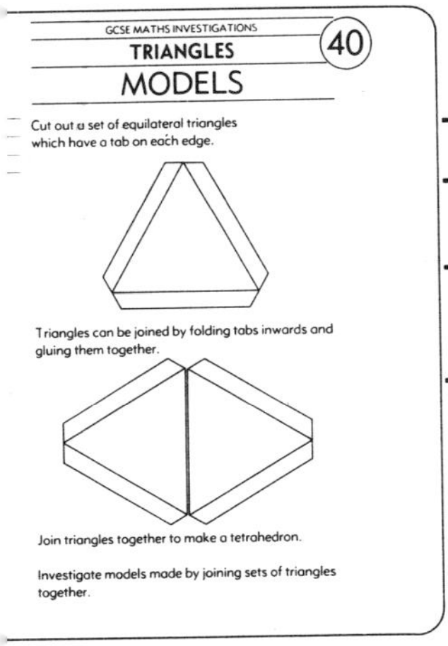
GCSE MATHS INVESTIGATIONS

TRIANGLES 40

MODELS

Cut out a set of equilateral triangles which have a tab on each edge.

Triangles can be joined by folding tabs inwards and gluing them together.

Join triangles together to make a tetrahedron.

Investigate models made by joining sets of triangles together.

GCSE MATHS INVESTIGATIONS

TRIANGLES

MODELS

40

Card
Scissors
Glue

△ A quick setting glue such as a glue stick is ideal. The lengths of sides of the triangles should be approximately 5 cm. These can be drawn using compasses, templates or they can be preduplicated on card.

△ with four triangles

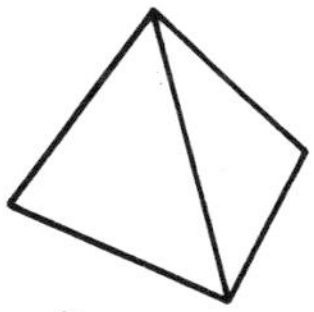

with six triangles

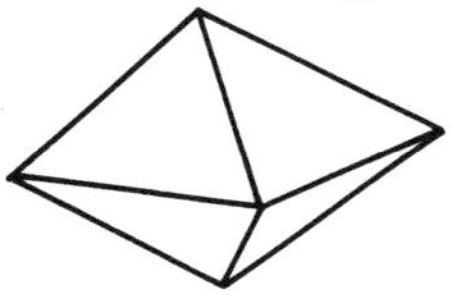

with eight triangles

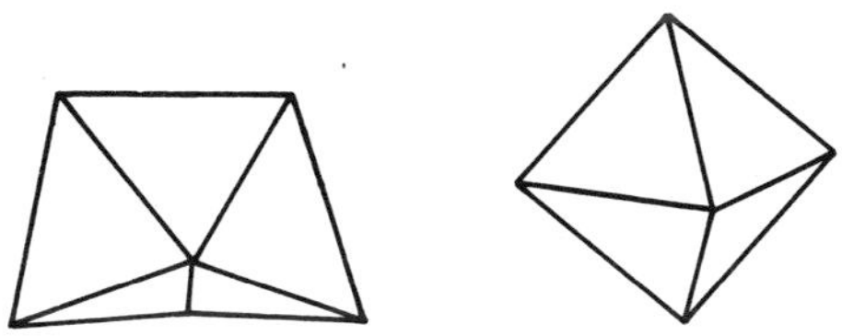

△ How many different models are possible with ten triangles?
Can a model be made with an odd number of triangles?
Can star shaped models be constructed?

△ Cut out other regular polygons with tabs on each edge.
Explore the construction of models using a combination of regular polygons:
e.g. squares and equilateral triangles.

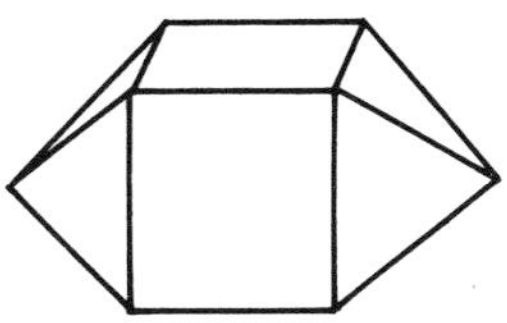

POWERS

	APPARATUS	ACTIVITY
41 End digits		Number patterns produced by end digits
42 Consecutive cubes		Summing consecutive cube numbers
43 Expressions		Creating numerical expressions for given numbers
44 Odds		Expressing odd numbers as the sum of primes and powers of two
45 Reverse squares	Calculator	Squaring numbers
46 Fibonacci squares		Squaring numbers in a Fibonacci series
47 Square differences		Expression of numbers as the difference between two square numbers
48 Generating primes	Table of primes	Exploring formulae for generating prime numbers

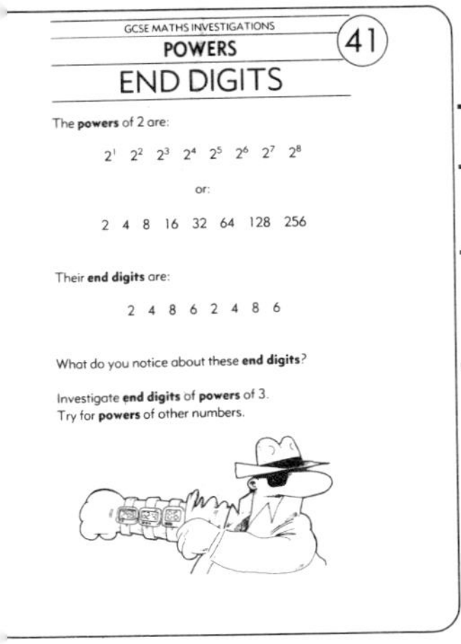
GCSE MATHS INVESTIGATIONS
POWERS
END DIGITS
41

The **powers** of 2 are:

2^1 2^2 2^3 2^4 2^5 2^6 2^7 2^8

or:

2 4 8 16 32 64 128 256

Their **end digits** are:

2 4 8 6 2 4 8 6

What do you notice about these **end digits**?

Investigate **end digits** of **powers** of 3.
Try for **powers** of other numbers.

GCSE MATHS INVESTIGATIONS

POWERS

END DIGITS

41

△ Powers of 2:
The end digits have a repeating cycle of 4 digits: 2 4 8 6

△ For which powers are the end-digits producing:
repeating cycles of 4 digits?
repeating cycles of 2 digits?
the same end digit all the time?

△ End digits for powers of other numbers can be tabulated:

powers of 3	3 9 7 1 3 9 7 1 . . . . .
powers of 4	4 6 4 6 4 6 4 6 . . . . .
powers of 5	5 5 5 5 5 5 5 5 . . . . .
powers of 6	6 6 6 6 6 6 6 6 . . . . .
powers of 7	7 9 3 1 7 9 3 1 . . . . .
powers of 8	8 4 2 6 8 4 2 6 . . . . .
powers of 9	9 1 9 1 9 1 9 1 . . . . .
powers of 10	0 0 0 0 0 0 0 0 . . . . .
powers of 11	1 1 1 1 1 1 1 1 . . . . .
powers of 12	2 4 8 6 2 4 8 6 . . . . .

△ The second powers (5^2, 7^2, ..) have these end digits:
4 9 6 5 6 9 4 1 0 1 4 ...
Which digits do or do not occur?
Investigate third powers, fourth powers, ...

△ Extend to end digits of powers in bases other than 10.

△ Explore end digits of other types of numbers: multiples of 3, square numbers.

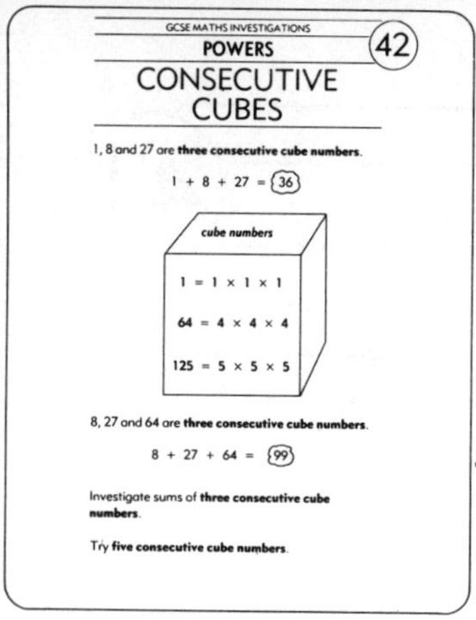
GCSE MATHS INVESTIGATIONS

POWERS (42)

CONSECUTIVE CUBES

1, 8 and 27 are **three consecutive cube numbers**.

1 + 8 + 27 = (36)

cube numbers

1 = 1 × 1 × 1

64 = 4 × 4 × 4

125 = 5 × 5 × 5

8, 27 and 64 are **three consecutive cube numbers**.

8 + 27 + 64 = (99)

Investigate sums of **three consecutive cube numbers**.

Try **five consecutive cube numbers**.

POWER (42)

CONSECUTIVE CUBES

△ The sums can be obtained from a table of cubes.

	cube numbers	sums of two consective cubes	sums of three consective cubes
1^3	1		36
2^3	8	9	99
3^3	27	35	216
4^3	64	91	405
5^3	125	189	684
6^3	216	341	1071
7^3	343	559	
8^3	512	855	
9^3	729		

$36 = 4 \times 9$
$99 = 11 \times 9$
$216 = 24 \times 9$
$405 = 45 \times 9$
$684 = 76 \times 9$
$1071 = 119 \times 9$

$(a + 1)^3 + a^3 + (a - 1)^3$
$= 3a^3 + 6a$
$= 3a(a^2 + 2)$

So, when $a = 2, 3a(a^2 + 2) = 36$
$a = 3, 3a(a^2 + 2) = 99$

Will they always be multiples of 9?

△

sums of two consecutive cubes	sums of three consective cubes	sums of five consecutive cubes
		225
9		440
35	36	775
91	99	1260
189	216	
341	405	
559	684	
855	1071	

$225 = 45 \times 5$
$440 = 88 \times 5$
$775 = 155 \times 5$
$1260 = 252 \times 5$

$(a + 2)^3 + (a + 1)^3 + a^3$
$+ (a - 1)^3 + (a - 2)^3$
$= 5a^3 + 30a$
$= 5a(a^2 + 6a)$

So, these will always be multiples of 5.

△ Explore the final digits of the numbers in the table.
For example, the final digits of the sums of two consecutive cubes are cyclic: 9, 5, 1, 9, 1

△ Try consecutive squares.

GCSE MATHS INVESTIGATIONS

POWERS

EXPRESSIONS

43

GCSE MATHS INVESTIGATIONS
POWERS
EXPRESSIONS
43

$a = 1, b = 2, c = 3$

Here are some **power expressions** for 8:

$8 = b^3$ one term

$8 = c^2 - a^2$ two terms

$8 = b^4 - c^2 + a^3$ three terms

Find some **power expressions** for other numbers.

Invent values for *e*, *f* and *g* and investigate **power expressions** using these values.

△ It is helpful to list the powers of a, b and c.

$a = 1$	$b = 2$	$c = 3$
$a^2 = 1$	$b^2 = 4$	$c^2 = 9$
$a^3 = 1$	$b^3 = 8$	$c^3 = 27$
$a^4 = 1$	$b^4 = 16$	$c^4 = 81$
$a^5 = 1$	$b^5 = 32$	$c^5 = 243$
$a^6 = 1$	$b^6 = 64$	$c^6 = 729$
$a^7 = 1$	$b^7 = 128$	$c^7 = 2187$

△ Decisions must be made about assumptions. For example, one power of each letter only is allowed in an expression. Assume that multiples of powers (e.g. $3b^2$) are not allowed.
A table can be drawn:

Number	One-term expression	Two-term expression	Three-term expression
1	a^2	$c^2 - b^3$	
2			
3		$b^2 - a^2$	
4	b^2		$b^5 - c^3 - a^2$
5		$c^2 - b^2$	
6			
7		$b^3 - a^2$	
8	b^3	$c^2 - a^2$	
⋮			

△ Is it possible to find a three-term expression for all numbers?

△ For which numbers can one-term, two-term and three-term expressions be found?

△ Try expressions based on $e = 3,\ f = 4,\ g = 5$.

△ Introduce negative values: $a = 2,\ b = -2,\ c = -3$

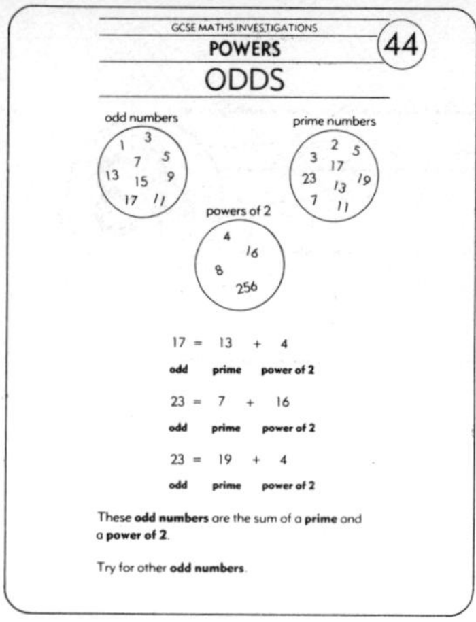
GCSE MATHS INVESTIGATIONS

POWERS 44

ODDS

odd numbers: 1 3 5 7 9 13 15 17 11

prime numbers: 2 3 5 17 23 13 19 7 11

powers of 2: 4 16 8 256

17 = 13 + 4
odd prime power of 2

23 = 7 + 16
odd prime power of 2

23 = 19 + 4
odd prime power of 2

These **odd numbers** are the sum of a **prime** and a **power of 2**.

Try for other **odd numbers**.

POWERS

ODDS

△ Every odd number can be expressed as the sum of a prime number and a power of two.

△ A table can be constructed:

Odd	Prime	Power of 2
1		
3	2	$1(2^0)$
5	3	$2(2^1)$
7	3	$4(2^2)$
9	5	$4(2^2)$
11	3	$8(2^3)$
13	11	$2(2^1)$
15	7	$8(2^3)$
17	13	$4(2^2)$
19	11	$8(2^3)$
21	5	$16(2^4)$
⋮	⋮	⋮

△ Some odd numbers can be expressed in more than one way:

$$\begin{aligned} 21 &= 19 + 2 \\ &= 17 + 4 \\ &= 13 + 8 \\ &= 5 + 16 \end{aligned} \qquad \begin{aligned} 11 &= 7 + 4 \\ &= 3 + 8 \end{aligned}$$

Investigate which numbers can be expressed in several ways.

△ Some even numbers can be expressed as the sum of a prime and a power of 3:

$$\begin{aligned} 8 &= 5 + 3 \\ 10 &= 7 + 3 \\ 12 &= 3 + 9 \\ 14 &= 11 + 3 \text{ or } 5 + 9 \\ 16 &= 7 + 9 \end{aligned}$$

Investigate further.

△ Investigate expressions for similar sums.

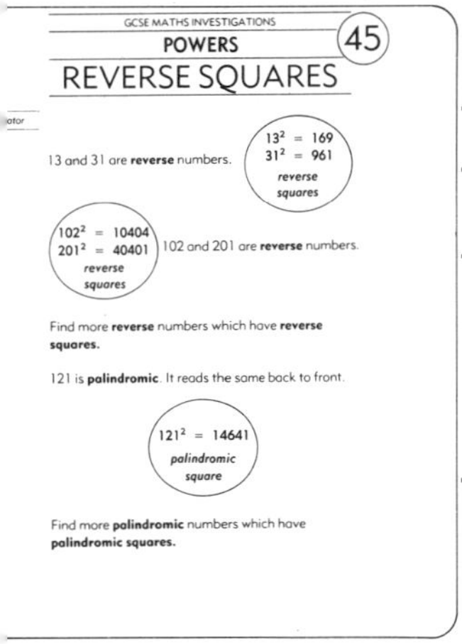
GCSE MATHS INVESTIGATIONS

POWERS (45)

REVERSE SQUARES

13 and 31 are **reverse** numbers.

$13^2 = 169$
$31^2 = 961$
reverse squares

$102^2 = 10404$
$201^2 = 40401$
reverse squares

102 and 201 are **reverse** numbers.

Find more **reverse** numbers which have **reverse squares.**

121 is **palindromic**. It reads the same back to front.

$121^2 = 14641$
palindromic square

Find more **palindromic** numbers which have **palindromic squares.**

GCSE MATHS INVESTIGATIONS

POWERS (45)

REVERSE SQUARES

Calculator

△ A trial and error method is likely at first. One could start by considering two-digit numbers, then three-digit, ... and so on.

△ Some solutions include:

Reverse squares		Palindronic squares
$12^2 = 144$	$21^2 = 441$	$11^2 = 121$
$13^2 = 169$	$31^2 = 961$	$22^2 = 484$
$102^2 = 10404$	$201^2 = 40401$	$101^2 = 10201$
$103^2 = 10609$	$301^2 = 90601$	$111^2 = 12321$
$112^2 = 12544$	$211^2 = 44521$	$121^2 = 14641$
$113^2 = 12769$	$311^2 = 96721$	$202^2 = 40804$
$122^2 = 14884$	$221^2 = 48841$	$212^2 = 44944$
$1002^2 = 1004004$	$2001^2 = 4004001$	$1001^2 = 1002001$
$1003^2 = 1006009$	$3001^2 = 9006001$	$1111^2 = 1234321$
$1012^2 = 1024144$	$2101^2 = 4414201$	
$1112^2 = 1236544$	$2111^2 = 4456321$	
$1122^2 = 1258884$	$2211^2 = 4888521$	
$1212^2 = 1468944$	$2121^2 = 4498641$	
$1031^2 = 1062961$	$1301^2 = 1692601$	
$1013^2 = 1026169$	$3101^2 = 9616201$	
$1103^2 = 1216609$	$3011^2 = 9066121$	
$1113^2 = 1238769$	$3111^2 = 9678321$	

△ For three–digit square numbers to have five digits, they must be less than $\sqrt{100,000} = 316.22776$ i.e. 316
So, for example, 321 (or 123) is too big.

△ An interesting pair of numbers is $1222^2 = 1493284$, $2221^2 = 4932841$.
Are there more like this?

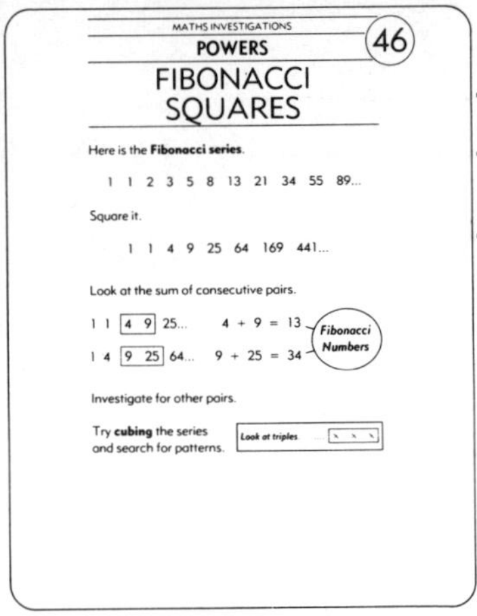
MATHS INVESTIGATIONS

POWERS (46)

FIBONACCI SQUARES

Here is the **Fibonacci series**.

1 1 2 3 5 8 13 21 34 55 89...

Square it.

1 1 4 9 25 64 169 441...

Look at the sum of consecutive pairs.

1 1 [4 9] 25... 4 + 9 = 13

1 4 [9 25] 64... 9 + 25 = 34

Fibonacci Numbers

Investigate for other pairs.

Try **cubing** the series and search for patterns.

Look at triples

GCSE MATHS INVESTIGATIONS

POWERS

46

FIBONACCI SQUARES

△ Consider the pairs in sequence:

$$\begin{aligned}
1^2 + 1^2 &= 2\\
1^2 + 2^2 &= 5\\
2^2 + 3^2 &= 13\\
3^2 + 5^2 &= 34\\
5^2 + 8^2 &= 89\\
8^2 + 13^2 &= 233
\end{aligned}$$

Summing these in order produces alternate terms in the original series.
If the Fibonacci series is labelled

$a_1, a_2, a_3, a_4, \ldots$

then a_n denotes the nth term of the series.

$$\begin{aligned}
\text{So } a_3^2 + a_4^2 &= a_7\\
a_4^2 + a_5^2 &= a_9\\
a_5^2 + a_6^2 &= a_{11}
\end{aligned}$$

and, generally, $a_n^2 + a_{n+1}^2 = a_{2n+1}$

So, summing the squares of the sixth and seventh terms, for example, produces the thirteenth term.

△ What is the **nineteenth** term of the series? Which terms when squared and summed will produce the **nineteenth** term?

△ The series 1 1 2 3 5 8 13 21 34 55 89 144 233 377 610...
cubed 1 1 8 27 125 512...

.. 1 [8 27 125] 512.. $125 + 27 - 8 = 144$ $a_5^3 + a_4^3 - a_3^3 = a_{12}$

8 [27 125 512] ... $512 + 125 - 27 = 610$ $a_6^3 + a_5^3 - a_4^3 = a_{15}$

and, generally, $a_{n+1}^3 + a_n^3 - a_{n-1}^3 = a_{3n}$

GCSE MATHS INVESTIGATIONS

POWERS (47)

SQUARE DIFFERENCES

$7 = 4^2 - 3^2$

$20 = 6^2 - 4^2$

$21 = 5^2 - 2^2$

7, 20 and 21 are expressed as the **difference between two square numbers**.

Can other numbers be expressed this way? Investigate.

GCSE MATHS INVESTIGATIONS

POWERS (47)

SQUARE DIFFERENCES

△ A difference table can be drawn:

	1	4	9	16	25	36	49	64	81	100
1	0	3	8	15	24	35	48	63	80	
4		0	5	12	21	32	45	60	77	
9			0	7	16	27	40	55	72	
16				0	9	20	33	48	65	
25					0	11	24	39	56	
36						0	13	28	45	
49							0	15	32	
64								0	17	
81									0	

△ Looking down the diagonals from top left to bottom right, the difference of squares of numbers that

(a) are consecutive, produces odd numbers (except 1)
examples: $3^2 - 2^2 = 5$, $4^2 - 3^2 = 7$, $5^2 - 4^2 = 9$...

(b) differ by 2, produces multiples of 4 (except 4)
examples: $3^2 - 1^2 = 8$, $4^2 - 2^2 = 12$, $5^2 - 3^2 = 16$...

(c) differ by 3, produces odd multiples of 3 (except 3, 9)
examples: $4^2 - 1^2 = 15$, $5^2 - 2^2 = 21$, $6^2 - 3^2 = 27$...

(d) differ by 4, produces multiples of 8 (except 8, 16)
examples: $5^2 - 1^2 = 24$, $6^2 - 2^2 = 32$, $7^2 - 3^2 = 40$...

△ Numbers which cannot be expressed as a square difference are:
1, 2, 4, 6, 10, 14, 18, 22, 26, 30, 34, 38, 42, ...
i.e. even numbers which are not multiples of 4 (numbers of the form $4n - 2$, where n is a positive integer) and 1 and 4.

△ Some numbers have several expressions. Is it possible to predict for a given number, how many different square differences are available?

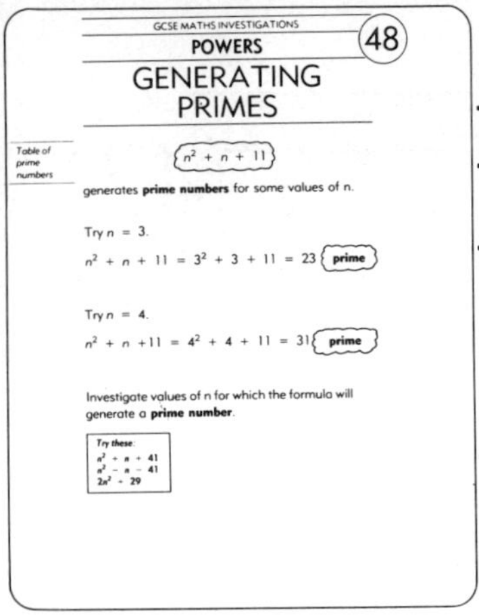

GCSE MATHS INVESTIGATIONS

POWERS

48

GENERATING PRIMES

△ A table is helpful: p = prime number

n	n^2	$n + n^2$	$n^2 + n + 11$	$n^2 + n + 41$	$n^2 - n + 41$	$2n^2 + 29$
0	0	0	11 p	41 p	41 p	29 p
1	1	2	13 p	43 p	41 p	31 p
2	4	6	17 p	47 p	43 p	37 p
3	9	12	23 p	53 p	47 p	47 p
4	16	20	31 p	61 p	53 p	61 p
5	25	30	41 p	71 p	61 p	79 p
6	36	42	53 p	83 p	71 p	101 p
7	49	56	67 p	97 p	83 p	127 p
8	64	72	83 p	113 p	97 p	157 p
9	81	90	101 p	131 p	113 p	191 p
10	100	110	121	151 p	131 p	229 p
11	121	132	143	173 p	151 p	271 p
12	144	156	167 p	197 p	173 p	317 p
13	169	182	193 p	223 p	197 p	367 p
14	196	210	221	251 p	223 p	421 p
15	225	240	521 p	281 p	251 p	479 p

△ Considering values of n where $0 \leqslant n \leqslant 15$:
$n^2 + n + 11$ fails when $n = 10, 11$ and 14
For what values does this expression fail when $n > 15$?
$n^2 + n + 41$, $n^2 - n + 41$ and $2n^2 + 29$ produce primes for all values of n in this range.
$n^2 + n + 41$ and $n^2 - n + 41$ generate the same prime numbers.

△ Is there any pattern in the position of the primes which are generated by each expression?

RECTANGLES

	APPARATUS	ACTIVITY
49 Domino	Squared paper Card	Symmetrical domino patterns based on square grids
50 Blanks	Squared paper Card	Arrangments of blank dominoes
51 Rectiles	Squared paper	Partitioning rectangles into smaller rectangles
52 Straight and tilted	Squared dotty paper	Investigating enclosed dots of different rectangles
53 Inners	Isometric dotty paper	Rectangles and enclosed dots
54 Crossings	Squared paper	Squares crossed by the diagonals of a rectangle
55 Counterpoint	Counters	Strategy puzzle based on moving counters into rectangular arrays
56 Blocks	Cubes	Volume and surface area of cuboids

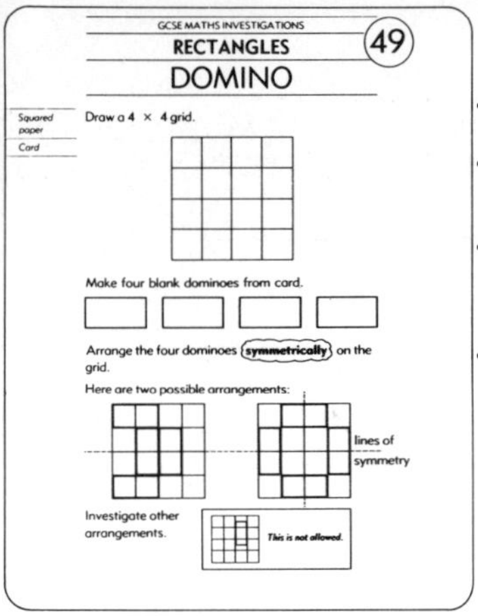
GCSE MATHS INVESTIGATIONS
RECTANGLES
DOMINO
49

Squared paper
Card

Draw a 4 × 4 grid.

Make four blank dominoes from card.

Arrange the four dominoes (symmetrically) on the grid.

Here are two possible arrangements:

Investigate other arrangements.

GCSE MATHS INVESTIGATIONS

RECTANGLES

DOMINO

49

Squared paper

Card

△ Symmetrical arrangements about a square. 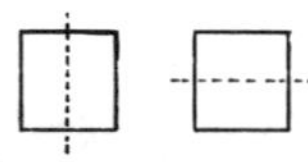
Some examples include:

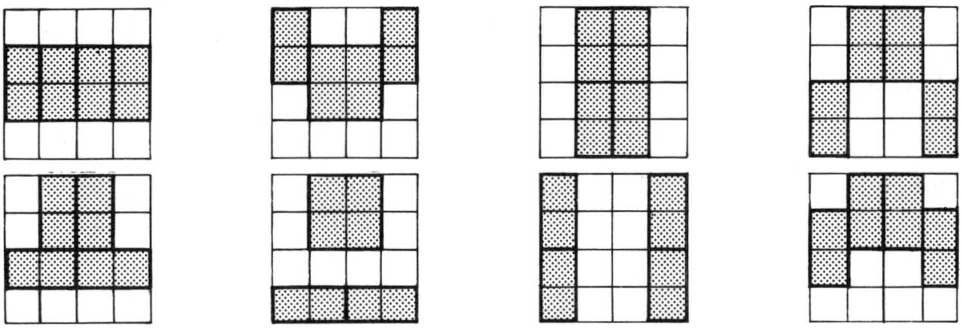

Which arrangements have more than one axis of symmetry?

△ Symmetrical arrangements about a square: 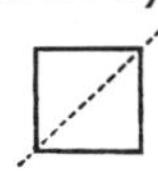
Examples include:

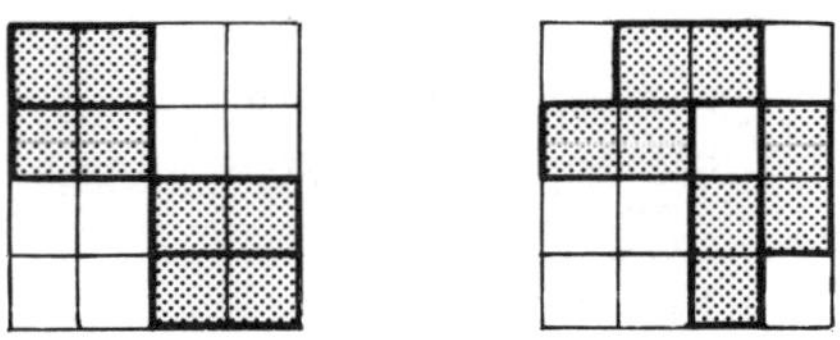

△ Arrangements having rotational symmetry:
Examples include:

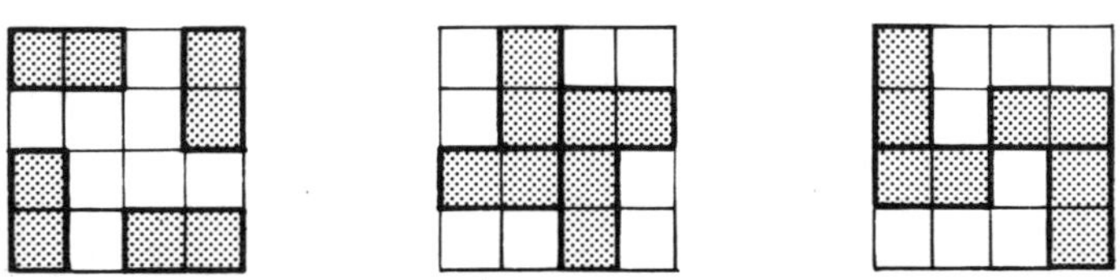

order four order four order two

△ Examine the shapes 'left' when the dominoes have been placed.
e.g. five squares one rectangle one octagon

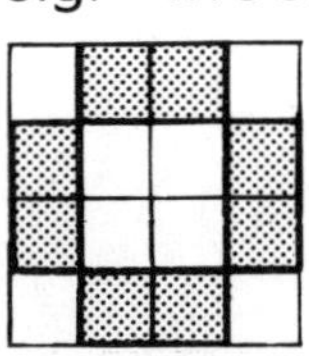

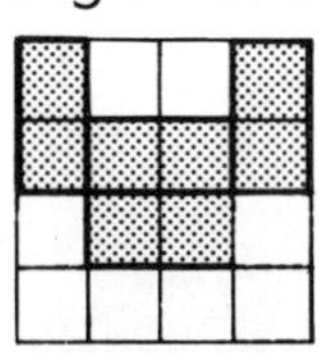

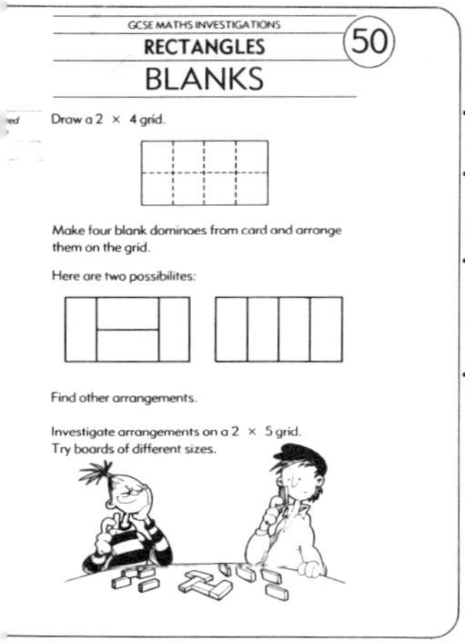
GCSE MATHS INVESTIGATIONS
RECTANGLES
BLANKS
50

Draw a 2 × 4 grid.

Make four blank dominoes from card and arrange them on the grid.

Here are two possibilities:

Find other arrangements.

Investigate arrangements on a 2 × 5 grid.
Try boards of different sizes.

GCSE MATHS INVESTIGATIONS

RECTANGLES

BLANKS

50

Squared paper
Card

△ 2 × 4 board – four dominoes. There are four possible solutions:

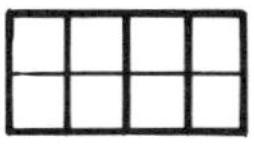
4 vertical

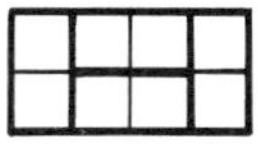
2 vertical,
2 horizontal

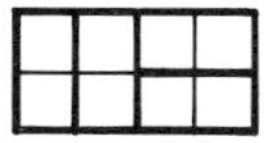
2 vertical,
2 horizontal,

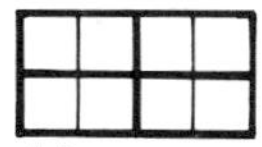
4 horizontal

△ 2 × 5 board – five dominoes. There are five solutions:

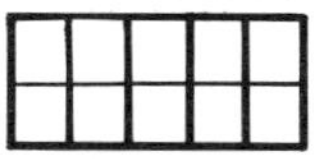
5 vertical

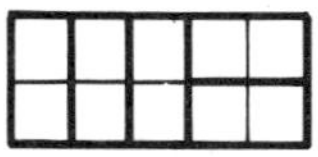
3 vertical
2 horizontal

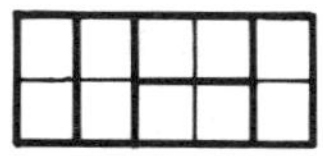
3 vertical,
2 horizontal

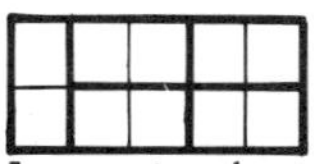
1 vertical,
4 horizontal

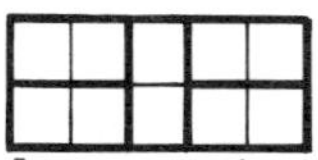
1 vertical,
4 horizontal

△ 2 × 5 board – four dominoes. Some solutions:

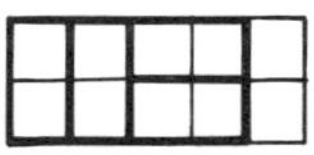

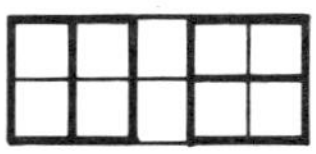

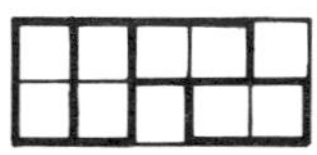

△ 2 × 6 board – six dominoes. There are eight solutions:

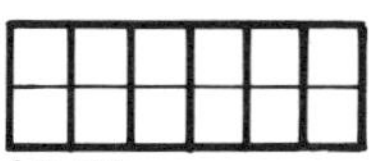
(6,0)

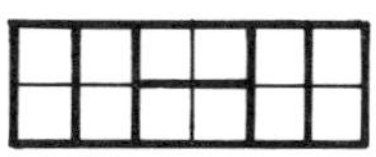
(4,2)

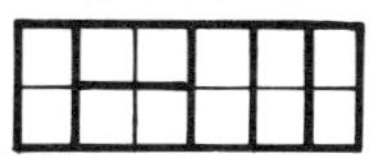
(4,2)

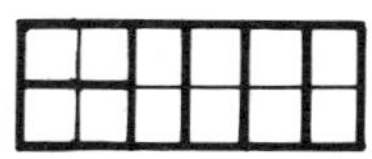
(4,2)

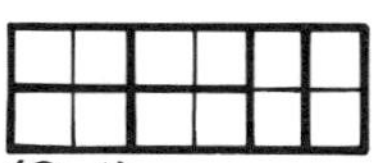
(2,4)

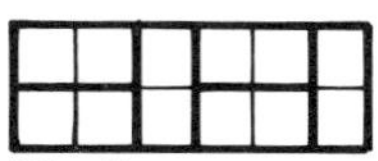
(2,4)

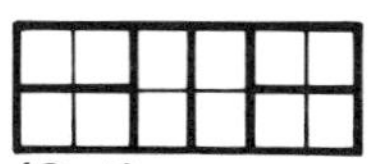
(2,4)

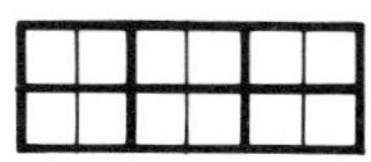
(0,6)

△ Is it possible to predict the number of solutions for a $2 \times n$ board?

△ Try for other size boards: 3 × 4

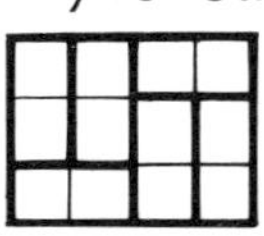

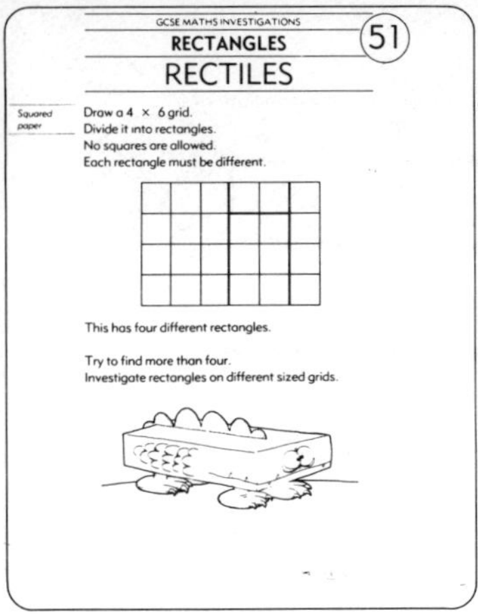
GCSE MATHS INVESTIGATIONS
RECTANGLES (51)
RECTILES

Squared paper

Draw a 4 × 6 grid.
Divide it into rectangles.
No squares are allowed.
Each rectangle must be different.

This has four different rectangles.

Try to find more than four.
Investigate rectangles on different sized grids.

GCSE MATHS INVESTIGATIONS

RECTANGLES

RECTILES

51

Squared paper

△ One strategy is to consider smaller grids first:

<u>2 × *n*</u> 2 × 2, 2 × 3. – impossible

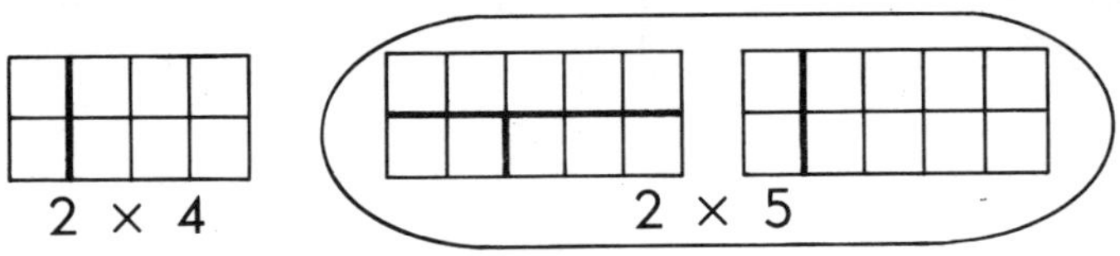

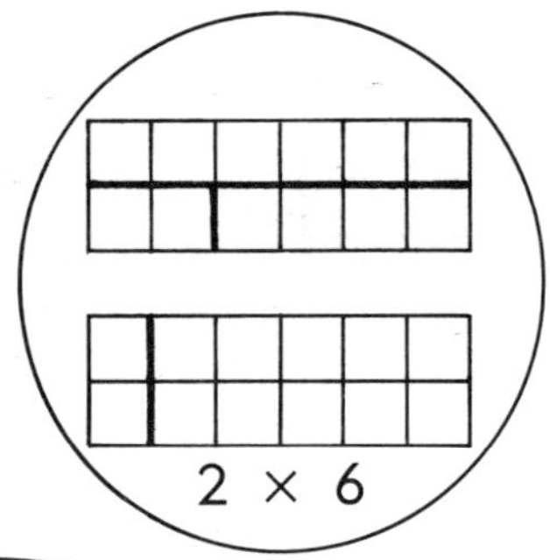

<u>3 × *n*</u> 3 × 2 – impossible

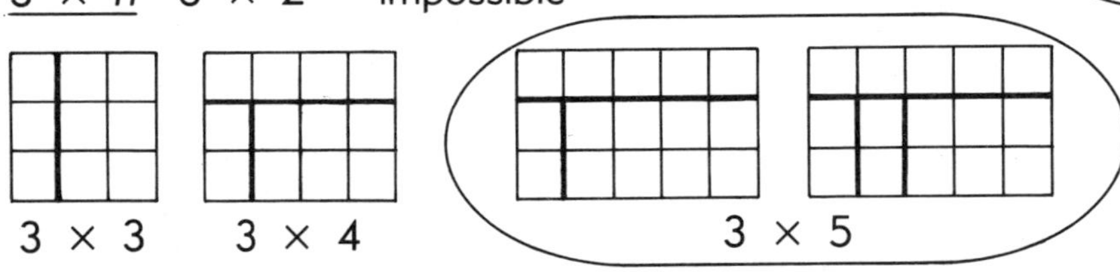

How many solutions can be found on a 3 × 6 grid?

<u>4 × 6</u> Here are nine different arrangements:

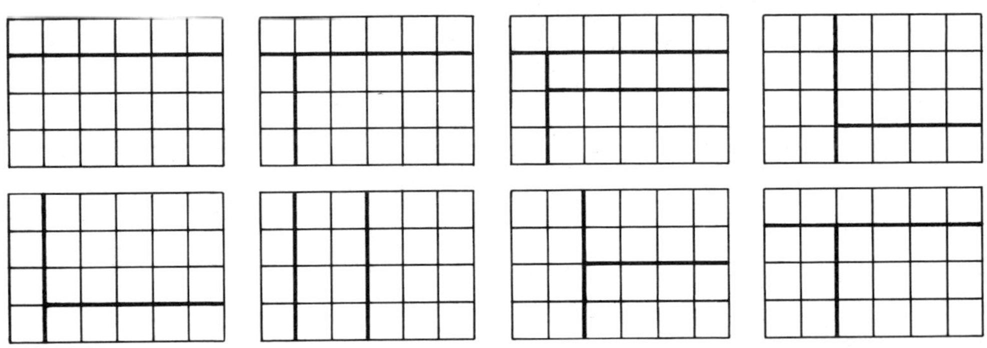

Are there any more solutions?
The last solution has five different rectangles.

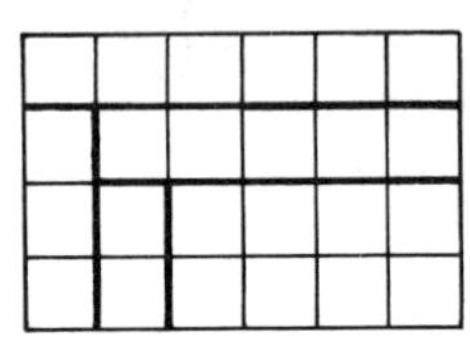

△ What is the smallest size of grid containing five different rectangles?

△ Investigate smallest size of grid containing six, seven, ... different rectangles.

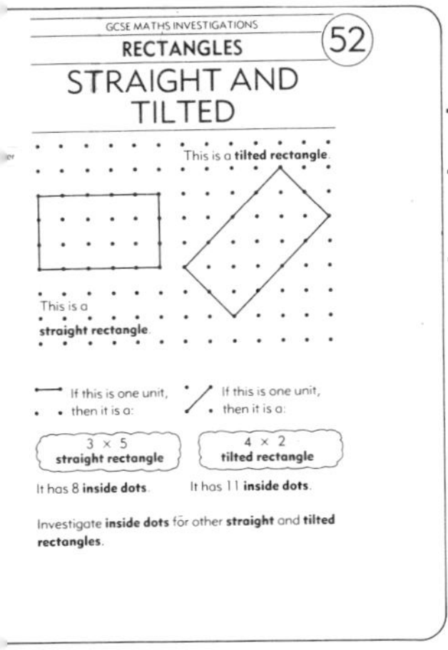
GCSE MATHS INVESTIGATIONS
RECTANGLES 52
STRAIGHT AND TILTED

This is a **tilted rectangle**.

This is a **straight rectangle**.

If this is one unit, then it is a:
3 × 5 **straight rectangle**
It has 8 **inside dots**.

If this is one unit, then it is a:
4 × 2 **tilted rectangle**
It has 11 **inside dots**.

Investigate **inside dots** for other **straight** and **tilted rectangles**.

GCSE MATHS INVESTIGATIONS

RECTANGLES

STRAIGHT AND TILTED

52

Dotty paper

△ Straight rectangles
It may be helpful to construct a table:

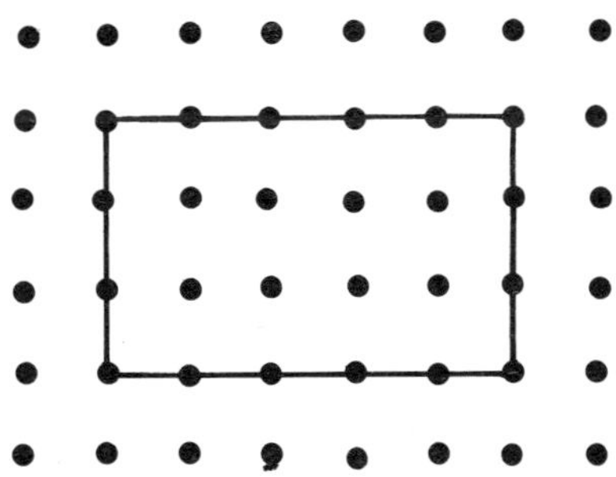

Rectangles	*Inside dots*
5 × 3	8
6 × 3	10
7 × 3	12
8 × 3	14
5 × 2	4
6 × 2	5
7 × 2	6
8 × 2	7
5 × 4	12
6 × 4	15

The number of inside dots is the product of one less than the length and one less than the width.
i.e. If the rectangle is $a \times b$,
then the number of inside dots is $(a - 1)\ (b - 1)$.

△ Tilted rectangles

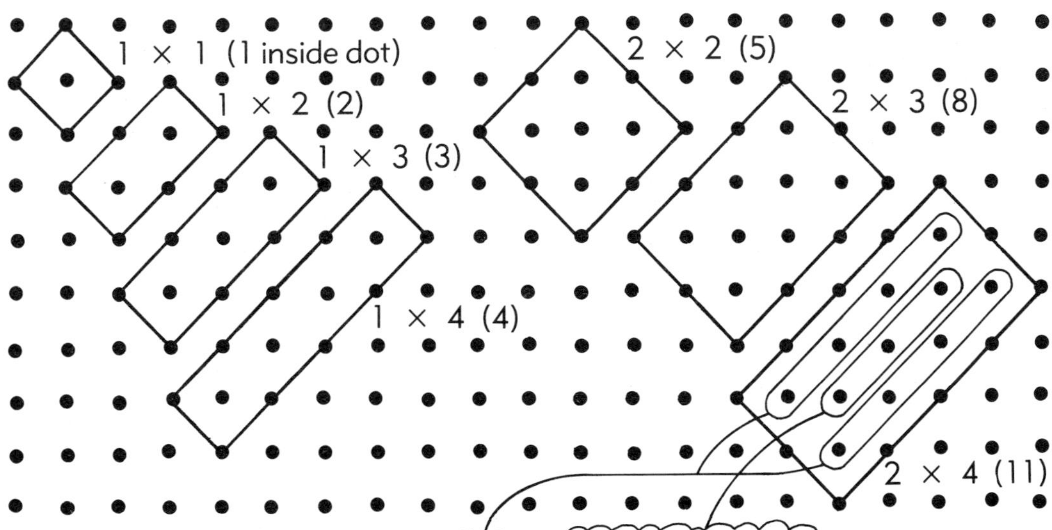

The number of inside dots is $a\ b + (a - 1)\ (b - 1)$.

△ Investigate rectangles tilted at angles other than 45°.

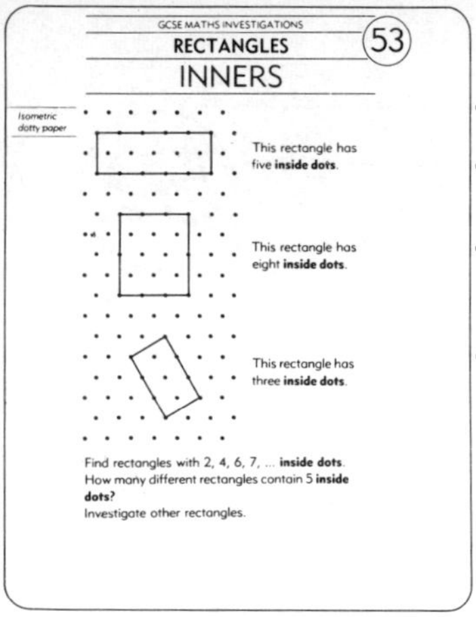
GCSE MATHS INVESTIGATIONS
RECTANGLES
INNERS
53

Isometric dotty paper

This rectangle has five **inside dots**.

This rectangle has eight **inside dots**.

This rectangle has three **inside dots**.

Find rectangles with 2, 4, 6, 7, ... **inside dots**.
How many different rectangles contain 5 **inside dots?**
Investigate other rectangles.

GCSE MATHS INVESTIGATIONS

RECTANGLES

INNERS

53

Isometric dotty paper

△ Some examples include:

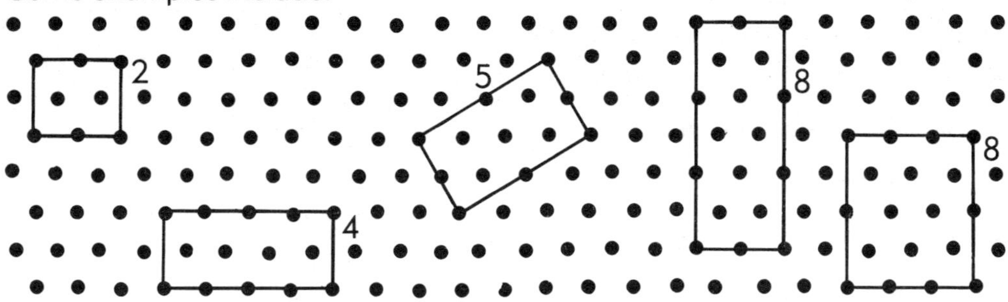

△ Note that

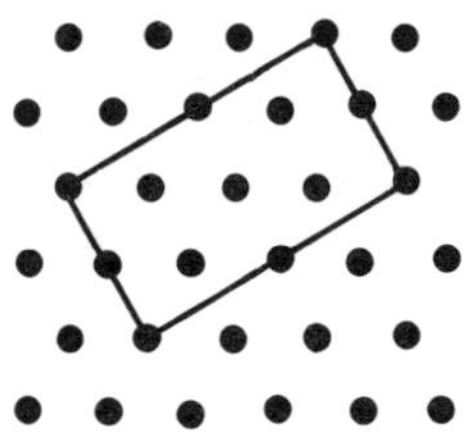

is merely a rotation of

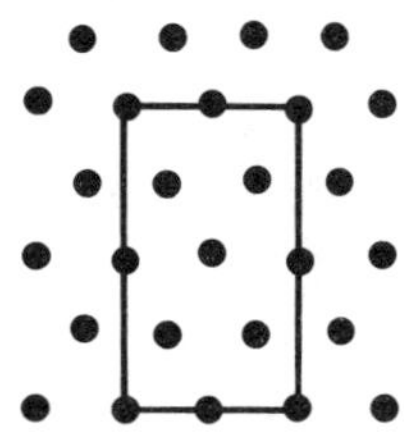

△ The dimensions of rectangles can be measured in terms of:

shorts 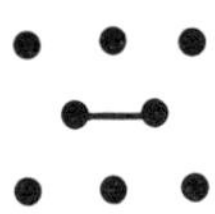 and longs  or (shorts × longs)

So, for example, 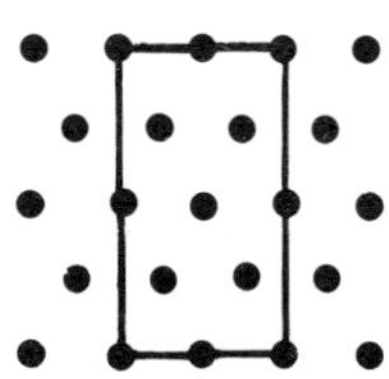 is a 2 × 2 rectangle.

△ For an $a \times b$ rectangle, the number of inside dots is $ab + (a - 1)(b - 1)$.
So, for example, rectangles with eight dots include:
$2 \times 3,\ 3 \times 2,\ 8 \times 1$

△ Explore the areas of the rectangles. Let 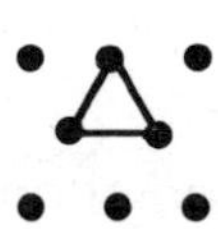 be 1 unit of area.

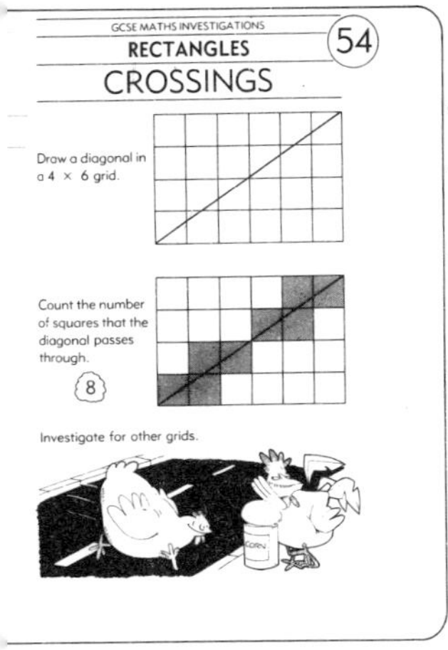

GCSE MATHS INVESTIGATIONS

RECTANGLES

CROSSINGS

54

Squared paper

△ One can start by trying some different grids:
$1 \times n,\ 2 \times n,\ 3 \times n, \ldots$

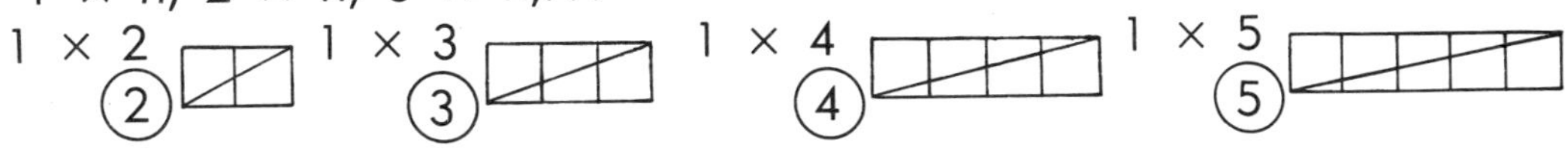

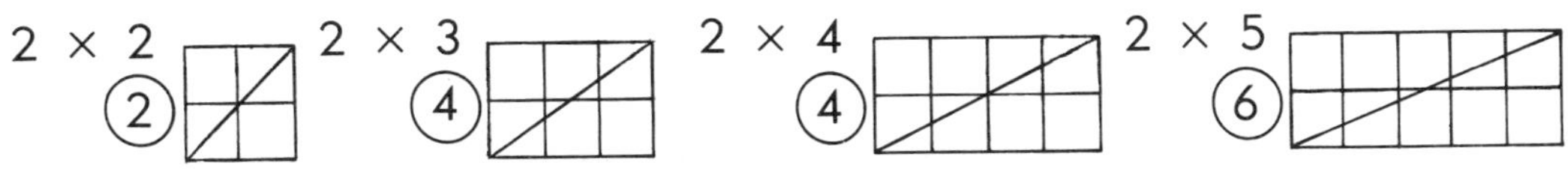

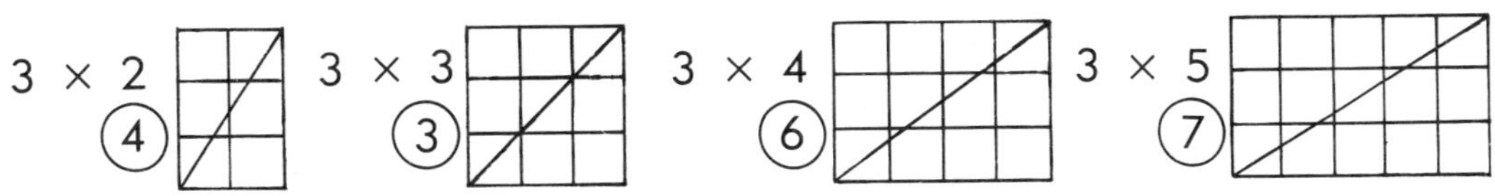

△ There is a relationship between a 4×6 grid and a 2×3 grid:

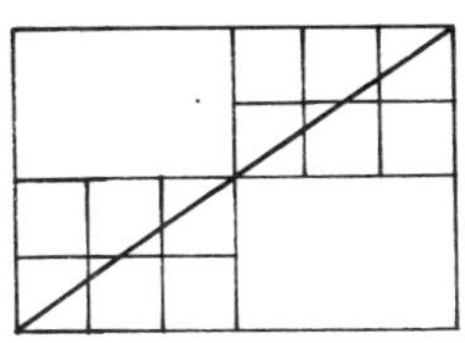

So, number of squares for a 4×6 grid is $2 \times$ (number of squares for a 2×3 grid).

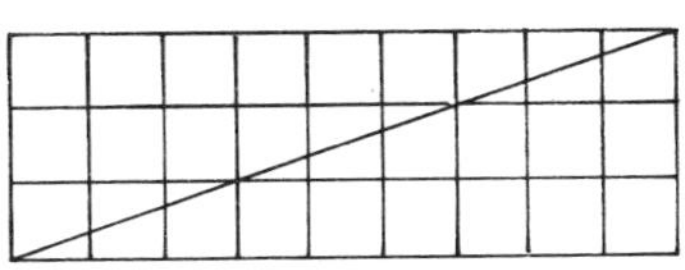

The number of squares for a 3×9 grid is $3 \times$ (number of squares for a 1×3 grid).

△ Generally, for an $a \times b$ grid:
If a, b have no common divisor, then number of squares crossed is $a + b - 1$.
If c is the highest common divisor of a and b, the number of squares crossed is

$$c\left(\frac{a}{c} + \frac{b}{c} - 1\right)$$

or $a + b - c$.

GCSE MATHS INVESTIGATIONS

RECTANGLES

COUNTERPOINT

55

Counters

△ Pupils can experiment with different methods of recording:

00
0000
000000
↓
0000
0000
0000
(2, 4, 6 → 1 move)

00
00000
00000
↓
0000
000
00000
↓
0000
000000
00
↓
0000
0000
0000
(2, 5, 5 → 3 moves)

0
000
00000000
↓
0
000000
00000
↓
00
000000
0000
↓
0000
0000
0000
(1, 3, 8 → 3 moves)

0
00000
000000
↓
00
0000
000000
↓
0000
0000
0000
(1, 5, 6 → 2 moves)

Starting Arrangement	*Moves*
1, 1, 10	4
1, 2, 9	3
1, 3, 8	3
1, 4, 7	2
1, 5, 6	2
2, 2, 8	2
2, 3, 7	3
2, 4, 6	1
2, 5, 5	3
3, 3, 6	impossible
3, 4, 5	2

Another way of recording the moves is:
(1, 2, 9) → (2, 2, 8) → (4, 2, 6) → (4, 4, 4)
(3, 4, 5) → (6, 4, 2) → (4, 4, 4)

△ Can you find a solution using 9 counters instead of 12?
What about 15 counters?

△ Solutions are available for even multiples of three only. Why?

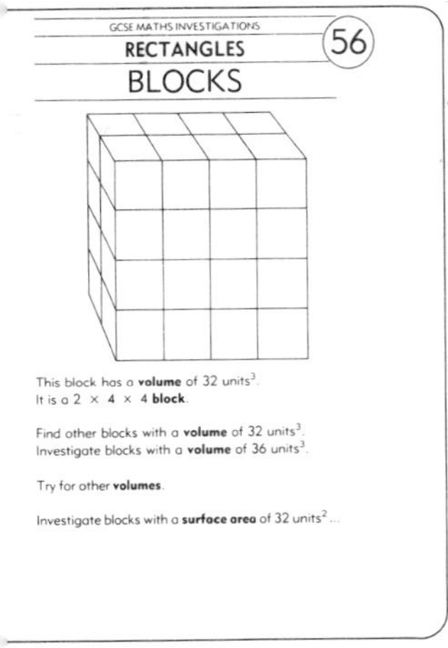
GCSE MATHS INVESTIGATIONS

RECTANGLES (56)

BLOCKS

This block has a **volume** of 32 units^3.
It is a $2 \times 4 \times 4$ **block**.

Find other blocks with a **volume** of 32 units^3.
Investigate blocks with a **volume** of 36 units^3.

Try for other **volumes**.

Investigate blocks with a **surface area** of 32 units^2...

GCSE MATHS INVESTIGATIONS

RECTANGLES (56)

BLOCKS

Cubes

△ Building blocks with cubes may be helpful.

△ 32 units^3. Solutions include $2 \times 4 \times 4$, $2 \times 2 \times 8$.
Several blocks exist with a dimension of 1 unit
e.g. $1 \times 4 \times 8$, $1 \times 2 \times 16$.

△ 36 units^3. One approach is to consider the prime factors of 36:
$2 \times 2 \times 3 \times 3$
This leads to the solutions:

$1 \times 2 \times 18$	$2 \times 2 \times 9$
$1 \times 4 \times 9$	$2 \times 3 \times 6$
$1 \times 3 \times 12$	$3 \times 3 \times 4$

Similarly, other volumes can be considered.
Which volume less than 100 units^3 has most blocks?

△ Surface area of 32 units^2: One possibility is $2 \times 2 \times 3$:

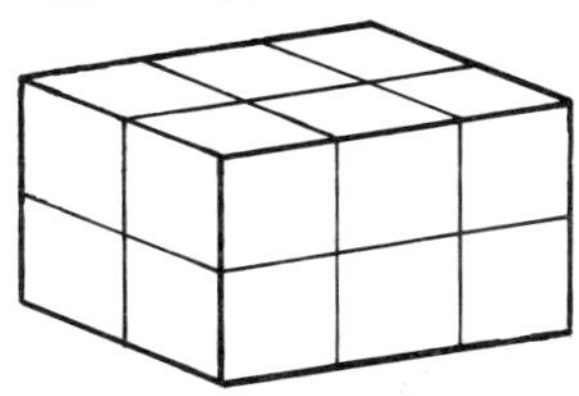

Are there any more?

△ Which surface area less than 50 units^2 has most blocks?

PATHS

	APPARATUS	ACTIVITY
57 Dotty paths	Dotty paper	Routes on 3 × 3 grids
58 Shunting		Arrangement from shunting trucks into sidings
59 Rollin	Square	Loci investigation
60 Jumping Jacks	Isometric dotty paper	Patterns on isometric paper
61 Knightly visits	Squared paper	Knight's moves on square grids
62 Billiards	2 cm squared paper	Rebounds on a rectangular billiard table
63 Journeys	Isometric dotty paper	Routes on a triangular grid
64 Factor ties		Factor chains

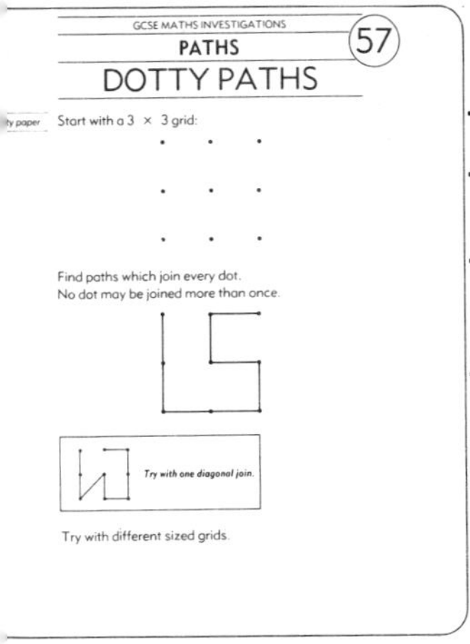
GCSE MATHS INVESTIGATIONS
PATHS
57
DOTTY PATHS
...ty paper
Start with a 3 × 3 grid:
Find paths which join every dot.
No dot may be joined more than once.
Try with one diagonal join.
Try with different sized grids.

GCSE MATHS INVESTIGATIONS

PATHS

DOTTY PATHS

57

Dotty paper

△ One approach is to consider all possible moves from a given starting point.

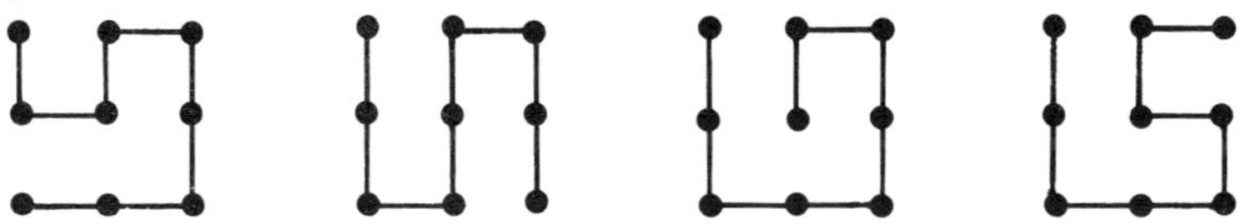

Starting vertically from point x, there are four different paths finishing at different points:

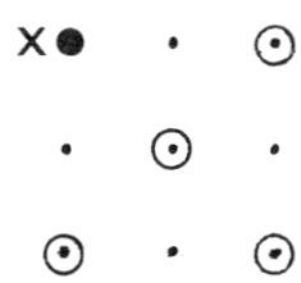

Consider the possible paths starting with a horizontal move from x.
Try starting from different positions on the grid.

△ If reflections and rotations are disallowed, how many paths from x now?

△ Try finding different paths where one diagonal move is allowed.

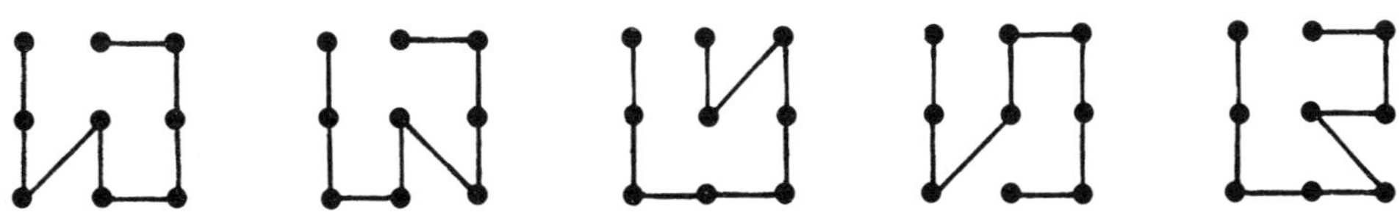

△ Investigate paths on different grids:

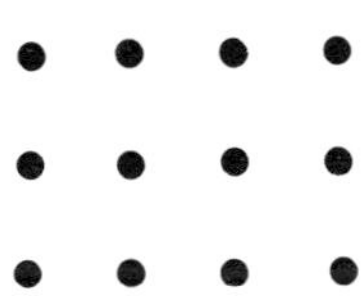

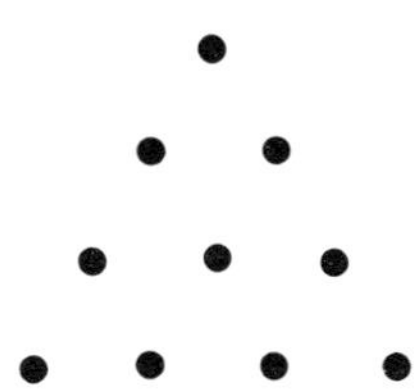

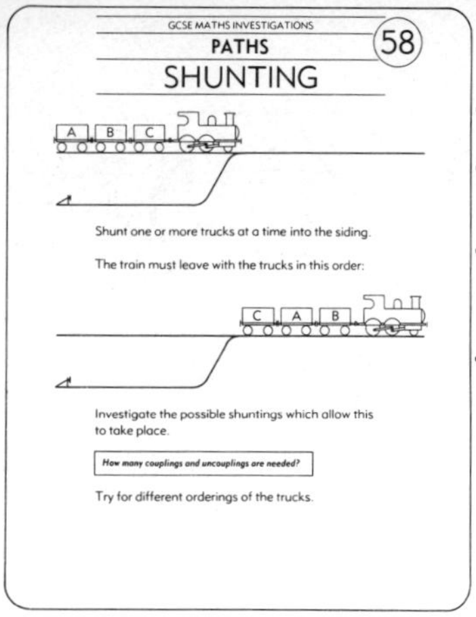

GCSE MATHS INVESTIGATIONS

PATHS

SHUNTING

58

- △ It may help to use lettered pieces of card.
- △ Examine the number of couplings and uncouplings which are needed:

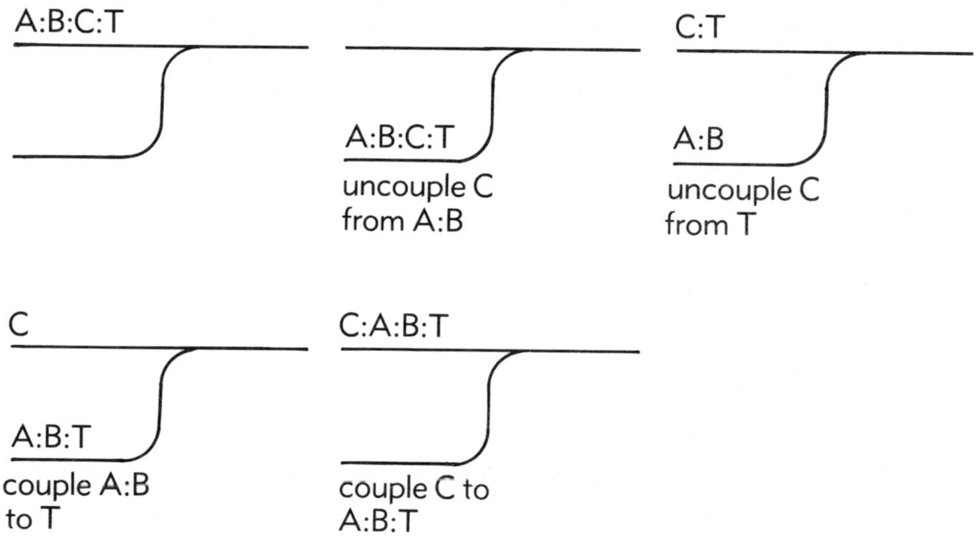

- △ How many couplings and uncouplings are needed to obtain the order A:C:B:T?
- △ Which order requires the maximum number of couplings and uncouplings?
- △ Try with a different number of trucks.
- △ Investigate different track layouts:

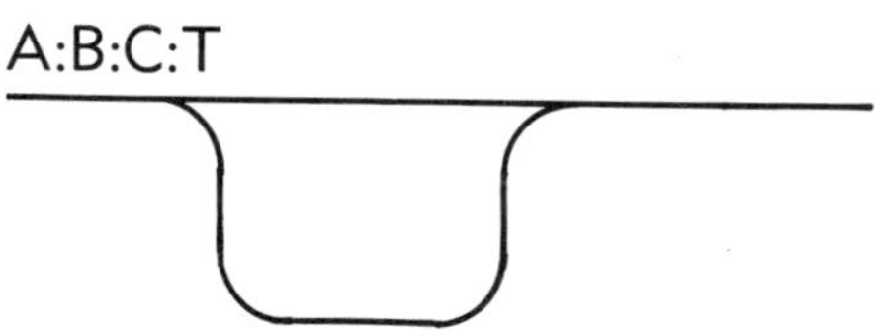

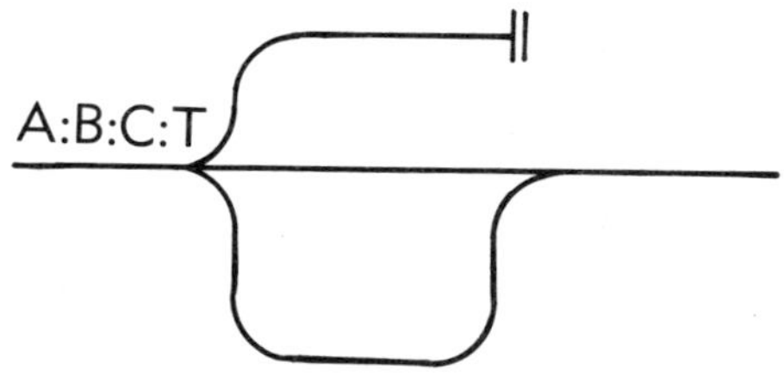

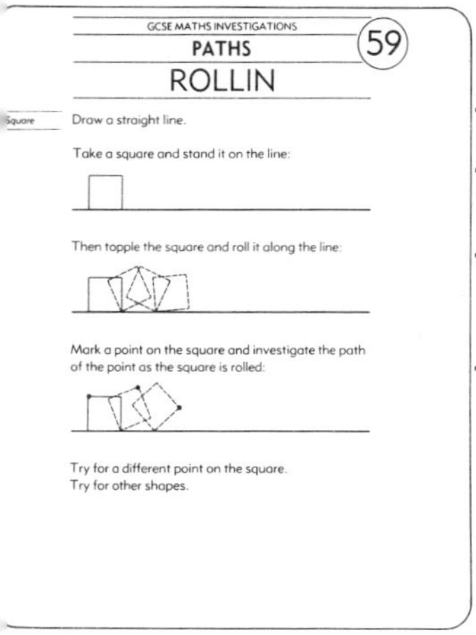

GCSE MATHS INVESTIGATIONS

PATHS

59

ROLLIN

Square

Draw a straight line.

Take a square and stand it on the line:

Then topple the square and roll it along the line:

Mark a point on the square and investigate the path of the point as the square is rolled:

Try for a different point on the square.
Try for other shapes.

GCSE MATHS INVESTIGATIONS

PATHS

ROLLIN

59

Square

△ Suppose the square is of side 1 unit. This path produces a pattern of quarter circles:
some of radius $\sqrt{2}$, and some of radius 1.

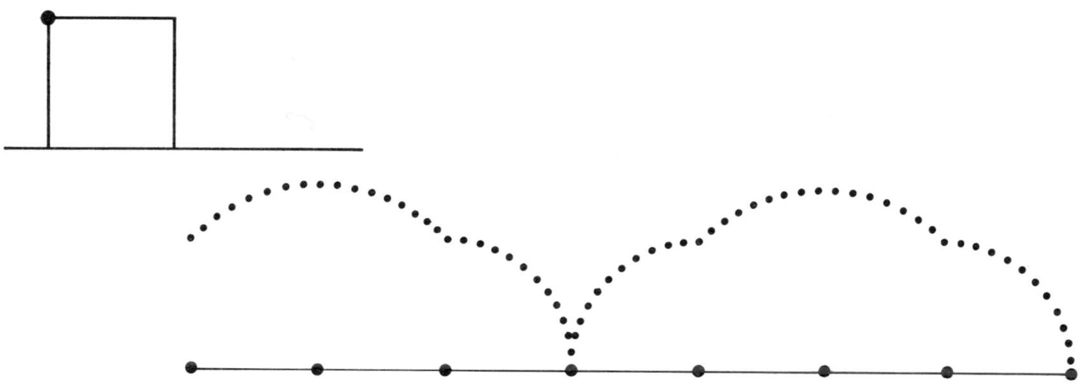

△ These quarter circles have radii of $\frac{\sqrt{3}}{2}$ and $\frac{1}{2}$.

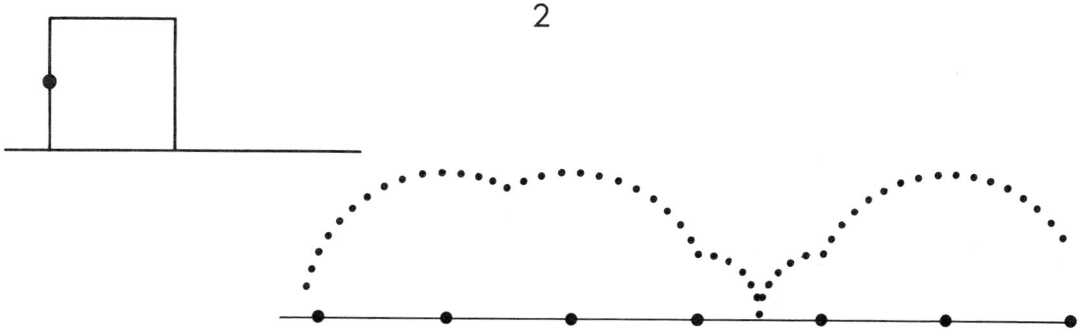

△ This pattern has only one size of quarter circle, of radius $\frac{\sqrt{2}}{2}$.

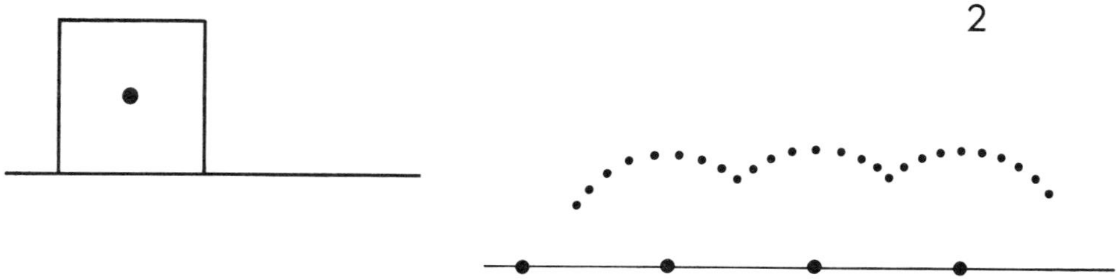

△ Try other positions on the square.

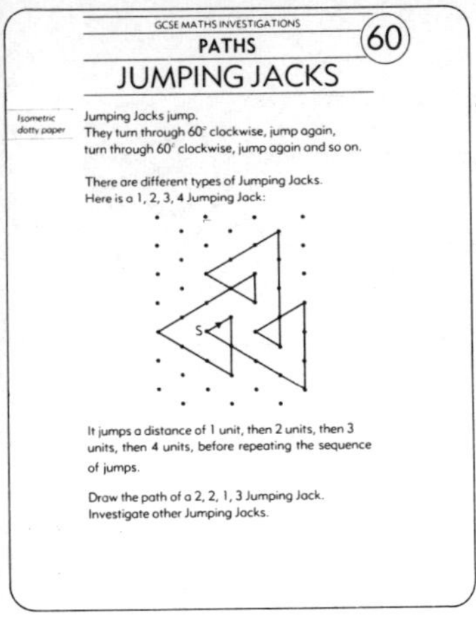
GCSE MATHS INVESTIGATIONS 60

PATHS

JUMPING JACKS

Isometric dotty paper

Jumping Jacks jump.
They turn through 60° clockwise, jump again, turn through 60° clockwise, jump again and so on.

There are different types of Jumping Jacks.
Here is a 1, 2, 3, 4 Jumping Jack:

It jumps a distance of 1 unit, then 2 units, then 3 units, then 4 units, before repeating the sequence of jumps.

Draw the path of a 2, 2, 1, 3 Jumping Jack.
Investigate other Jumping Jacks.

PATHS (60)

JUMPING JACKS

Isometric dotty paper

△ Does any sequence of four numbers produce a closed loop?

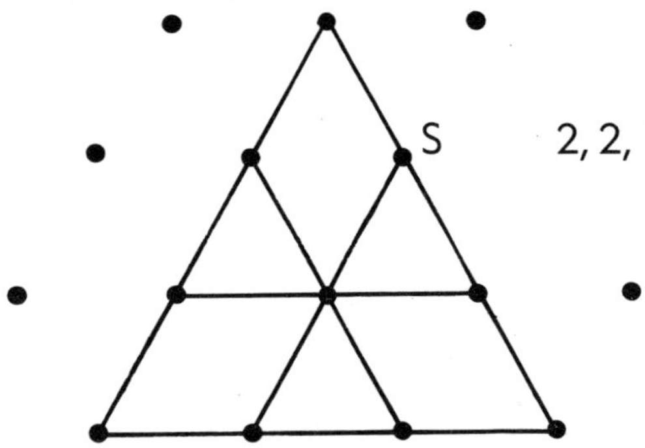

2, 2, 1, 1, Jumping Jack

△ Does the order in which the numbers are used make a difference?
△ What happens if three or five numbers are used?
△ The use of some anticlockwise jumps produces interesting patterns.

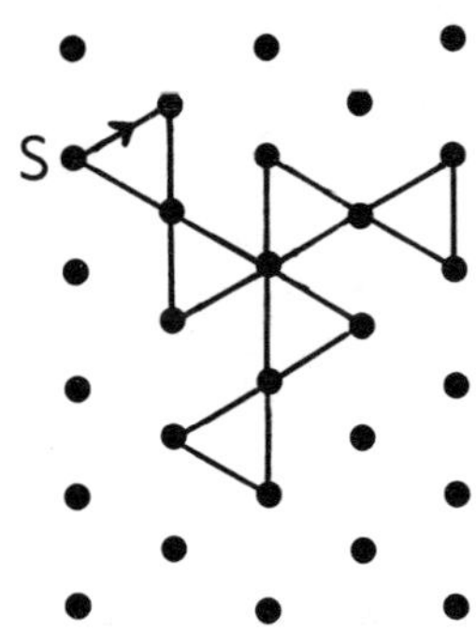

1,2, −3, Jumping Jack

△ Investigate Jumping Jacks on squared dotty paper.

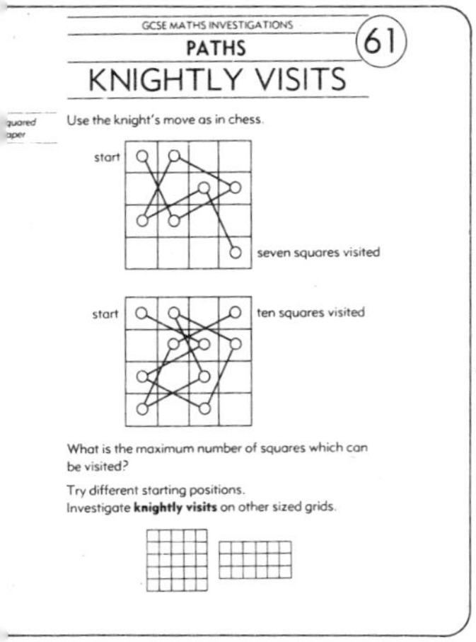
GCSE MATHS INVESTIGATIONS

PATHS

61

KNIGHTLY VISITS

Use the knight's move as in chess.

start

seven squares visited

start

ten squares visited

What is the maximum number of squares which can be visited?

Try different starting positions.

Investigate **knightly visits** on other sized grids.

GCSE MATHS INVESTIGATIONS

PATHS

KNIGHTLY VISITS

61

Squared paper

△ On a 4 × 4 grid the maximum number of squares which can be visited is 15.

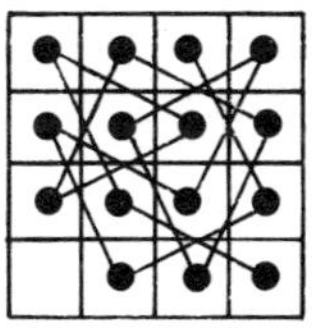

This can also be shown by numbering the squares:

13	10	1	6
4	7	12	9
11	14	5	2
	3	8	15

△ Try a 5 × 5 grid:

1	14	9	20	3
24	19	2	15	10
13	8	23	4	21
18	25	6	11	16
7	12	17	22	5

All the squares can be visited.

△ Try rectangles:

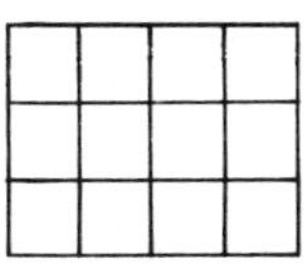

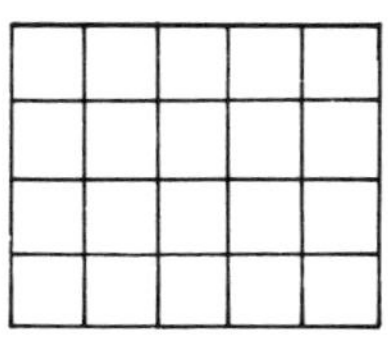

△ Try different grids:

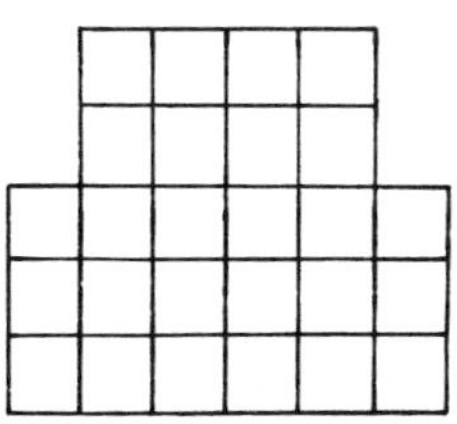

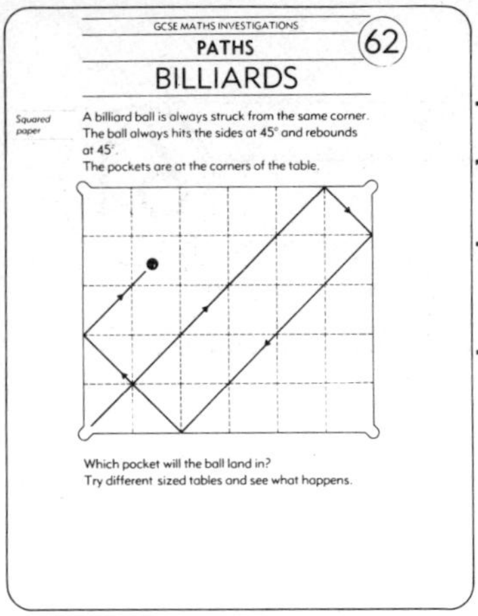
GCSE MATHS INVESTIGATIONS

PATHS (62)

BILLIARDS

Squared paper

A billiard ball is always struck from the same corner.
The ball always hits the sides at 45° and rebounds at 45°.
The pockets are at the corners of the table.

Which pocket will the ball land in?
Try different sized tables and see what happens.

GCSE MATHS INVESTIGATIONS

PATHS

BILLIARDS

62

2 cm squared paper

△ One possible approach would be to consider 1 × *n* tables, then 2 × *n* tables.

△ The number of rebounds can be tabulated:

	1	2	3	4	5	6	7	8	9	10
1	0	1	2	3	4	5	6	7	8	9
2	1	0	3	1	5	2	7	3	9	4
3	2	3	0	5	6	1	8	9	2	11
4	3	1	5	0	7	3	9	1	11	5
5	4	5	6	7	0	9	10	11	12	1
6	5	2	1	3	9	0	11	5	3	6
7	6	7	8	9	10	11	0	13	14	15

△ Which sized tables allow the ball to pass through each square? When will the ball enter the bottom right-hand pocket?

△ Can the number of rebounds be generalized for any given table?

△ Instead of the 45° rule, what would happen if the ball could hit other points around the table and the angle of rebound equalled the angle of impact?

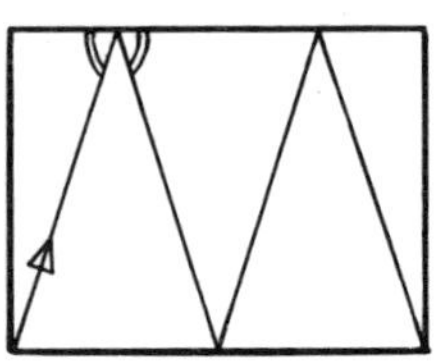

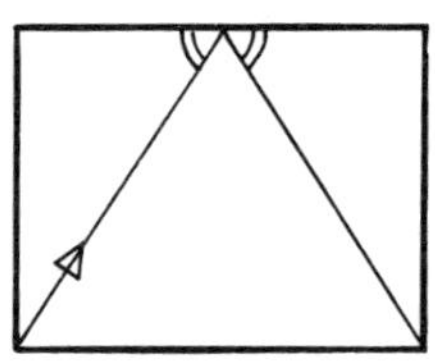

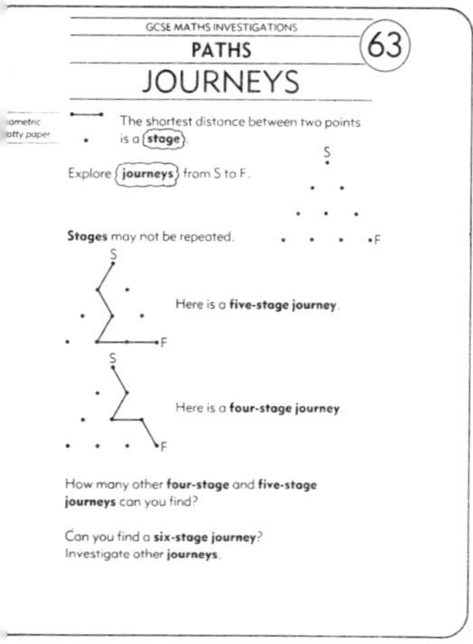
GCSE MATHS INVESTIGATIONS
PATHS
63
JOURNEYS

The shortest distance between two points is a (stage).

Explore (journeys) from S to F.

Stages may not be repeated.

Here is a **five-stage journey**.

Here is a **four-stage journey**.

How many other **four-stage** and **five-stage journeys** can you find?

Can you find a **six-stage journey**?
Investigate other **journeys**.

GCSE MATHS INVESTIGATIONS

PATHS

JOURNEYS

63

Isometric dotty paper

△ Four-stage journeys: There are five.

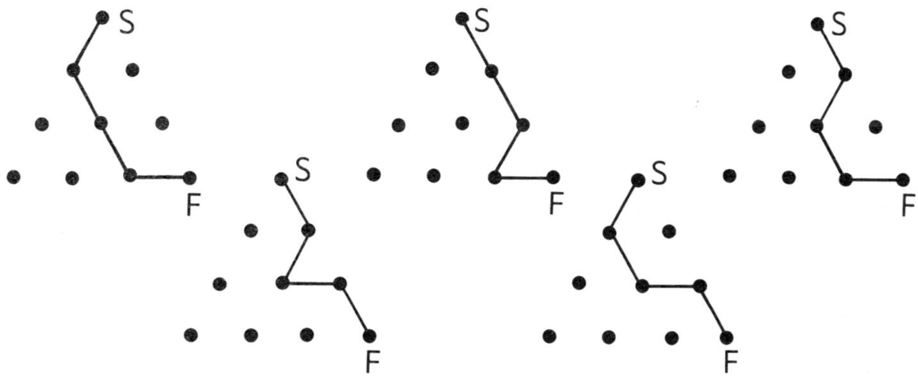

△ Five-stage journeys:
One strategy for finding these is to consider different two-stage starts:

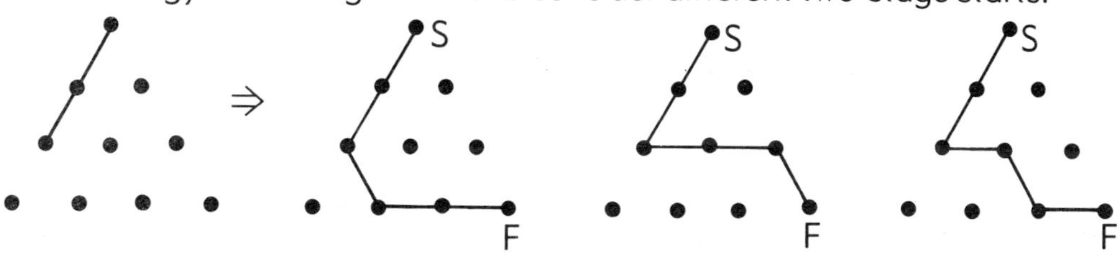

△ Other two-stage starts are:

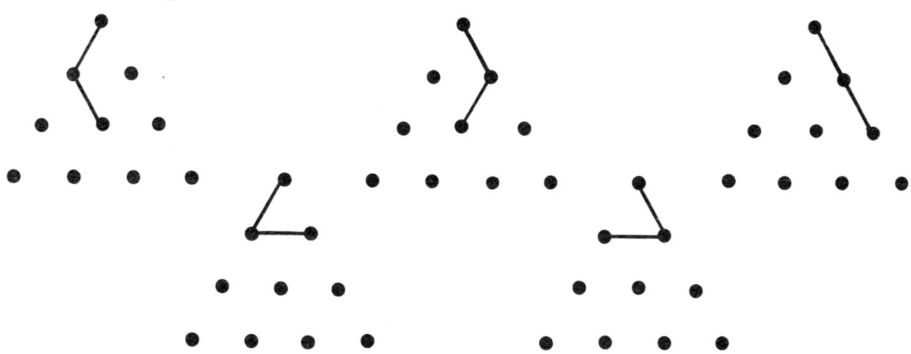

△ What is the longest possible journey?

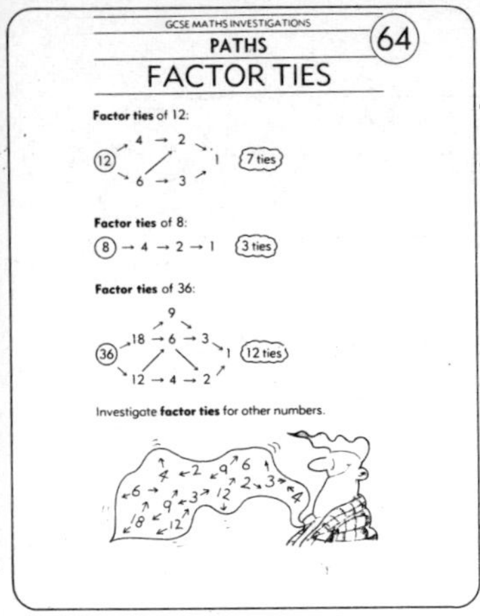

GCSE MATHS INVESTIGATIONS

PATHS

FACTOR TIES

64

△ Prime numbers (i.e. numbers with 2 divisors) have 1 tie:
2, 3, 5, 7, 11, 13, 17, 19, ... (19) → 1

△ Powers of 2: 2^n has n ties:
(32) → 16 → 8 → 4 → 2 → 1

△ Powers of 3: 3^n has n ties:
(27) → 9 → 3 → 1

△ Numbers with 3 divisors have 2 ties:
4, 9, 25, 49, ... ◯ → ◯ → 1

△ Numbers with 4 divisors have 4 ties:
6, 10, 8, 38, 22, 15, 34, ...

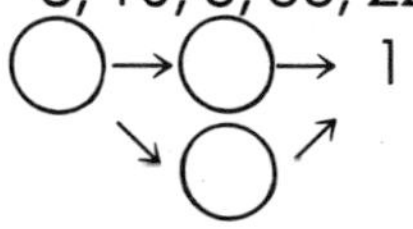

6 → 2 → 1
↘ 3 ↗

22 → 11 → 1
↘ 2 ↗

△ Numbers with 6 divisors have 7 ties:
12, 18, 20, 28, 32, 44, 45, 50, ...

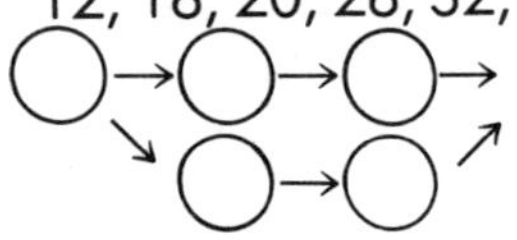

20 → 4 → 2 → 1
↘ 10 ⇉ 5 ↗

44 → 4 → 2 → 1
↘ 22 ⇉ 11 ↗

N.B. not 32 (power of 2)

△ Numbers with 8 divisors seem to fall into two categories:
24, 30, 40, 42

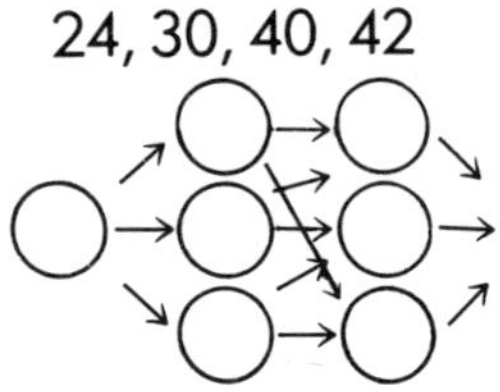

1 (12 ties)

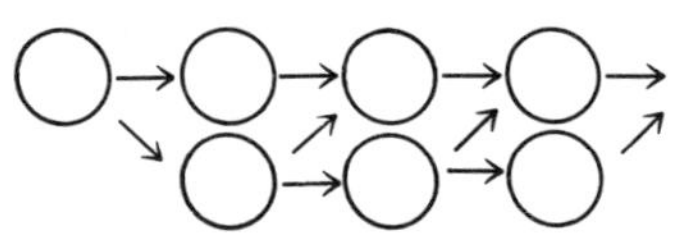

(10 ties)

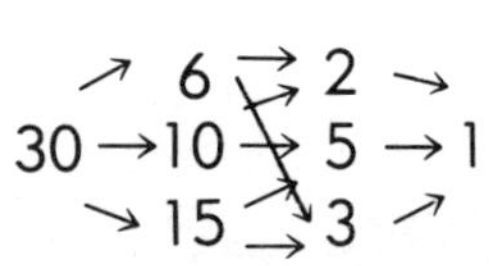

40 → 8 → 4 → 2 → 1
↘ 20 ⇉ 10 ⇉ 5 ↗

NUMBER

	APPARATUS	ACTIVITY
65 Five steps		Fibonacci series
66 Content numbers		Number properties based on divisors
67 Opening pairs		Fibonacci series
68 Oxo	Calculator Table of primes Table of squares	Three-figure palindromic numbers
69 Thirty-two		Expressions based on a restricted set of digits
70 Divisors		Patterns in numbers and their number of divisors
71 Intervals		Fibonacci series
72 Instructions	Table of primes	Creation of "Think of a Number" problems

Cards 65, 67, 71, in addition to card 46, relate to investigations based on the based on the Fibonacci series.

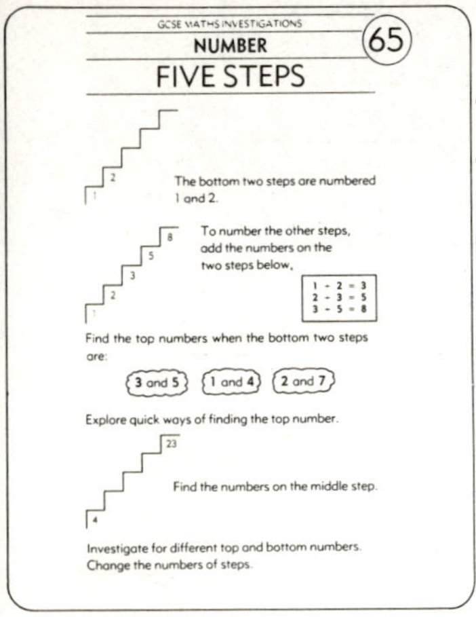

GCSE MATHS INVESTIGATIONS

NUMBER 65

FIVE STEPS

The bottom two steps are numbered 1 and 2.

To number the other steps, add the numbers on the two steps below.

1 + 2 = 3
2 + 3 = 5
3 + 5 = 8

Find the top numbers when the bottom two steps are:

3 and 5 | 1 and 4 | 2 and 7

Explore quick ways of finding the top number.

Find the numbers on the middle step.

Investigate for different top and bottom numbers. Change the numbers of steps.

NUMBER

65

FIVE STEPS

△ If a and b are the bottom numbers, then $2a + 3b$ is the top number.

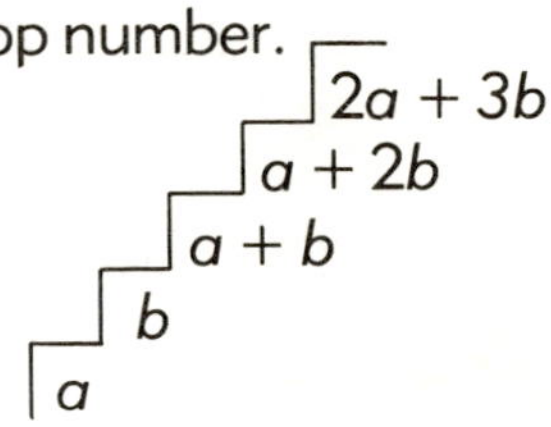

So, if $a = 3$, $b = 5$, top number is $2(3) + 3(5) = 21$
if $a = 1$, $b = 4$, top number is $2(1) + 3(4) = 14$
if $a = 2$, $b = 7$, top number is $2(2) + 3(7) = 26$

△ 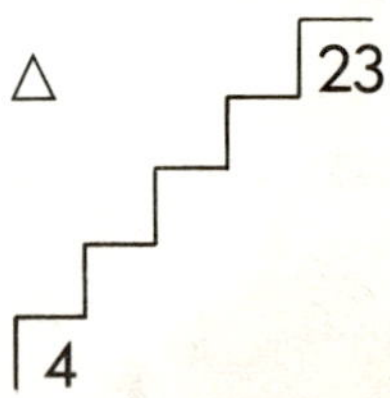

If $2a + 3b = 23$
and $a = 4$
then $3b = 23 - 8$
$= 15$
$\Rightarrow b = 5$

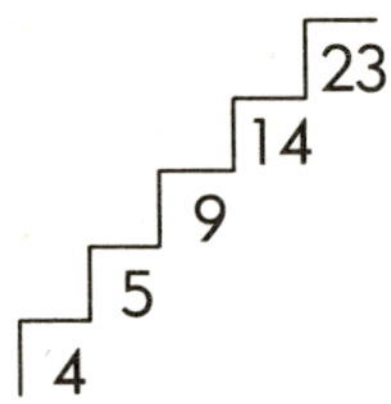

△ If 23 is the top number, how many integer solutions are there?

If $a = 1$, $b = 7$
$a = 2$, $b = 6\frac{1}{3}$
$a = 3$, $b = 5\frac{2}{3}$
$a = 4$, $b = 5$
$a = 5$, $b = 4\frac{1}{3}$
$a = 6$, $b = 3\frac{2}{3}$
$a = 7$, $b = 3$
$a = 8$, $b = 2\frac{1}{3}$
$a = 9$, $b = 1\frac{2}{3}$
$a = 10$, $b = 1$
$a = 11$, $b = \frac{1}{3}$

There are four solutions:

The solutions can be shown graphically:

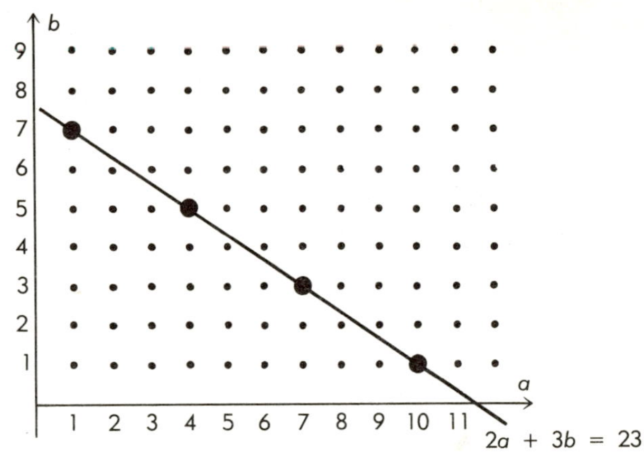

△ Consider five-step integer solutions having other top numbers:

24 → (3, 6), (9, 2), (6, 4)
25 → (2, 7), (5, 5), (8, 3), (11, 1)
26 → (1, 8), (4, 6), (7, 4), (10, 2)

These solutions can be illustrated by drawing lines parallel to $2a + 3b = 23$ on the graph.

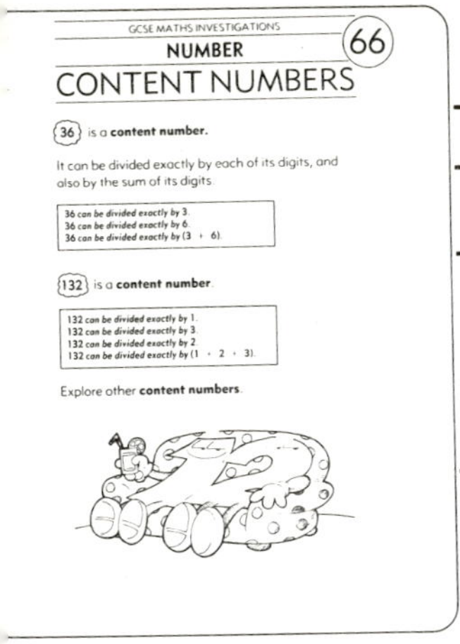
GCSE MATHS INVESTIGATIONS

NUMBER

66

CONTENT NUMBERS

(36) is a **content number.**

It can be divided exactly by each of its digits, and also by the sum of its digits.

36 can be divided exactly by 3.
36 can be divided exactly by 6.
36 can be divided exactly by (3 + 6).

(132) is a **content number**.

132 can be divided exactly by 1.
132 can be divided exactly by 3.
132 can be divided exactly by 2.
132 can be divided exactly by (1 + 2 + 3).

Explore other **content numbers**.

CONTENT NUMBERS

△ Content numbers include the single-digit numbers:

1, 2, 3, 4, 5, 6, 7, 8, 9

△ Some two-digit content numbers are:

12 (It can be divided by 1, 2 and 3.)
24 (It can be divided by 2, 4 and 6.)
36 (It can be divided by 3, 6 and 9.)

△ Are all multiples of 12 content?

△ Are there any content numbers which are not multiples of 12?

△ Some three-digit content numbers are:

144 (It can be divided by 1, 4 and 9.)
111 (It can be divided by 1 and 3.)
112 (It can be divided by 1, 2 and 4.)
How many three-digit content numbers exist?

△ Investigate **smug** numbers.

A **smug** number can be divided exactly by each of its digits and also by the product of its digits.
(36) is **smug** since it can be divided exactly by 3, 6 and 18 (3 × 6).

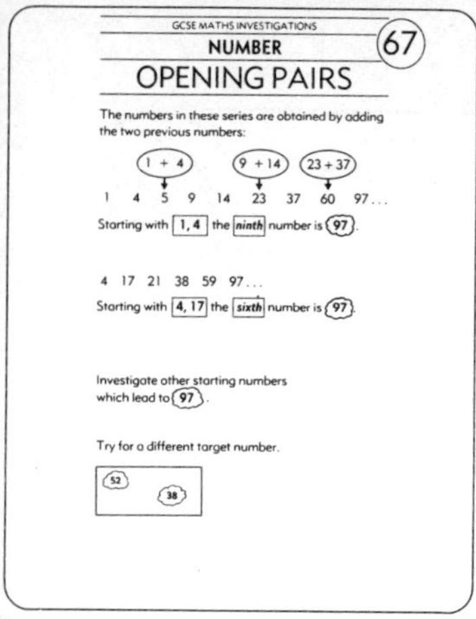
GCSE MATHS INVESTIGATIONS
NUMBER
67
OPENING PAIRS

The numbers in these series are obtained by adding the two previous numbers:

1 + 4 9 + 14 23 + 37

1 4 5 9 14 23 37 60 97...

Starting with 1, 4 the *ninth* number is 97.

4 17 21 38 59 97...

Starting with 4, 17 the *sixth* number is 97.

Investigate other starting numbers which lead to 97.

Try for a different target number.

52 38

NUMBER 67

OPENING PAIRS

△ One possible approach is to work backwards:
try 97 61
This leads to 97 61 36 25 11 14
Thus, 97 is the **sixth** in a series starting with 14, 11.
is the **fifth** in a series starting with 11, 25 etc.
In some of the series, the first two terms are not always in ascending order.

△ Suppose a and b are the starting numbers:

1	4	5	9	14	23	37	60	97
a	b	$a+b$	$a+2b$	$2a+3b$	$3a+5b$	$5a+8b$	$8a+13b$	$13a+21b$

97 is the ninth term in the series, and is a solution to the equation
$13a + 21b = 97$ i.e. $a = 1$, $b = 4$.
There are no other positive integer solutions to this equation, so no other series has 97 as the ninth term.

△ What about non-integer solutions?

△ Consider the possibility of 97 as the **seventh** term:
We require solutions to $5a + 8b = 97$.
We can search for solutions by taking values of b, in order:

b	1	2	3	4	5	6	7	8	9	10	11	12
$5a$	89	81	73	65	57	49	41	33	25	17	9	1
a				13					5			

Thus, we have two integer solutions:
$a = 13$, $b = 4$: 13 4 17 21 38 59 97
$a = 5$, $b = 9$: 5 9 14 23 37 60 97

△ 97 as the **eighth** term: only one solution → 4 5 9 14 23 37 60 97

△ 97 as the **sixth** term: six solutions:

29	2	31	33	64	97
24	5	29	34	63	97
19	8	27	35	62	97
14	11	25	36	61	97
9	14	23	37	60	97
4	17	21	38	59	97

△ Which is the longest series? (1, 3)?

△ Extend to other target numbers.

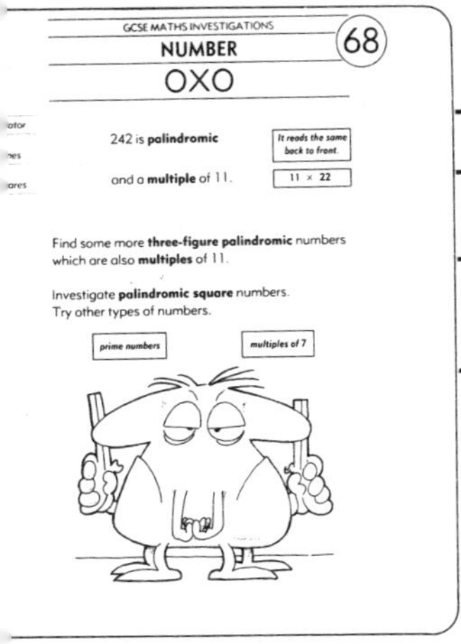

GCSE MATHS INVESTIGATIONS

NUMBER (68)

OXO

△ There are 90 three-figure palindromic numbers:

101	202	303	404 ...	909
111	212	313	414	919
121	222	323	424	929
131	232	333	434	939
141	242	343	444	949
151	252	353	454	959
161	262	363	464	969
171	272	373	474	979
181	282	383	484	989
191	292	393	494	999

△ Multiples of 11: 121, 242, 363, 484, 616, 737, 858, 979
△ Cubic numbers: 343
△ Square numbers: 121 (11^2), 484 (22^2), 676 (26^2)
note: 11 and 22 are palindromic
△ Triangluar numbers: 171, ...
△ One approach to investigating a particular type of number is to list them: multiples of 7

105 112 119 126 133 140 147 154 (161) 168 175 182 189 196
203 210 217 224 231 238 245 (252) 259 266 273 280 287 294
301 308 315 322 329 336 (343) 350 357 364 371 378 385 392 399
406 413 420 427 (434)

So, multiples of 7 are: 161, 252, 343, ...
△ Which palindromic numbers are prime numbers?

GCSE MATHS INVESTIGATIONS
NUMBER (69)
THIRTY-TWO

Use the digits 2, 3, 4, 5 and 6.
Each digit can be used **once only** in an expression.

Here are some expressions for (32):

34 − 2
64 − 32
(5 × 6) + 2
4 × (5 + 3)

How many other expressions can you find for (32)?
Try for some other numbers.

GCSE MATHS INVESTIGATIONS

NUMBER

THIRTY-TWO

69

△ Many different expressions are possible.
These can be categorised according to the operations used:
addition, subtraction, powers

$23 + 4 + 5$
$24 + 3 + 5$
$25 + 3 + 4$
$26 + 4 + 5 - 3$

$34 - 2$
$36 - 4$
$56 - 24$
$64 - 32$

$64 \div 2$
$35 - (6 \div 2)$
$(56 \div 2) + 4$

$4 \times (3 + 5)$
$4 \times (2 + 6)$

2^5
$2^3 \times 4$
$4^3 - 2^5$
$5^2 + 3 + 4$
$6^2 - 4$

$36 - 2 - \sqrt{4}$
$(5 \times 6) + \sqrt{4}$
$(6 \times \sqrt{25}) + \sqrt{4}$
$8\sqrt{4} \times 2$
$2\sqrt{4} \times 8$

$4! + 6 + 2$
$4! + 3! + 2!$
$(6 \times 3!) - 4$
$(5 \times 3!) + 2$

△ Investigate which combinations of operations provide solutions:
For example, $(\times, +)$: $4 \times (3 + 5)$
$(\div, +)$: $(56 \div 2) + 4$

△ Groups of pupils may choose a target number and compete to find the most solutions.

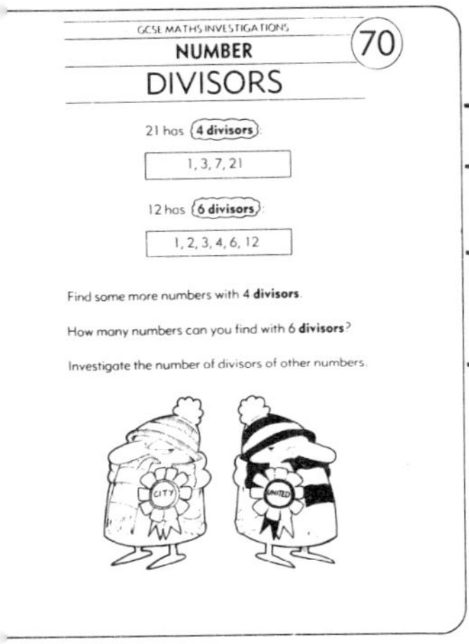
GCSE MATHS INVESTIGATIONS
NUMBER
70
DIVISORS

21 has **4 divisors**

1, 3, 7, 21

12 has **6 divisors**

1, 2, 3, 4, 6, 12

Find some more numbers with 4 **divisors**.

How many numbers can you find with 6 **divisors**?

Investigate the number of divisors of other numbers.

GCSE MATHS INVESTIGATIONS

NUMBER

DIVISORS

70

△ The number of divisions of each number can be tabulated:

Number	*Divisors*	*Total*
10	1 2 5 10	4
11	1 11	2
12	1 2 3 4 6 12	6
13	1 13	2
14	1 2 7 14	4
⋮		⋮

△ Sets with a given number of divisors can then be considered:

(2) 2, 3, 5, 7, 11, 13, 17, 19, 23, ...
(3) 4, 9, 25, 49, ...
(4) 6, 8, 10, 14, 15, 21, 22, 26, ...
(5) 16, 81, ...
(6) 12, 18, 20, 28, 32, 44, 45, ...
(7) 64, ...
(8) 24, 30, 40, 42, ...
(9) 36, 100, ...

△ Two divisors → prime numbers
Odd number of divisors → square numbers
Three divisors → squares of prime numbers.

△ What are numbers with 5 divisors, 11 divisors, ...?

△ Given a particular number, is it possible to state its number of divisors?

△ Find five numbers with 3 divisors, 5 divisors, ...

GCSE MATHS INVESTIGATIONS

NUMBER (71)

INTERVALS

Table of primes

Start with any pair of numbers: (1, 2)

The numbers in the series are found by adding the two previous numbers.

(3 + 5) (13 + 21)

1 2 3 5 8 13 21 34 55 89 ....
O E O O E O O E O O

Look at the pattern of **odd** numbers:

0 – 0 0 – 0 0 – 0 0 ....

Investigate the patterns of other numbers.

odd numbers even numbers prime numbers multiple of 3

Try for different pairs of starting numbers.

GCSE MATHS INVESTIGATIONS

NUMBER (71)

INTERVALS

△ Odds/evens

(a) starting O E

1	2	3	5	8	13	21	34	55	89	...
O	E	O	O	E	O	O	E	O	O	...

3	8	11	19	30	49	79	128	...
O	E	O	O	E	O	O	E	...

(b) starting E O → the same result

2	3	5	8	13	...
E	O	O	E	O	...

(c) starting O O → the same result

3	5	8	13	21	...
O	O	E	O	O	...

(d) starting E E

2	6	8	14	22	36	...
E	E	E	E	E	E	...

△

	1	2	3	5	8	13	21	34	55	89	144	233	377	610	987	...
primes		p	p	p		p						p				
multiples			×3				×3				×3				×3	
				×5					×5					×5		

Multiples of three and five occur at regular intervals.
What other patterns can be found?
Do the starting numbers make any difference?

△

	1	3	4	7	11	18	29	47	76	123	199	322	521	843	1364
primes		p		p	p		p	p			p		p		
multiples		×3				×3				×3				×3	

Again, a regular pattern for multiples of three results.
This sequence has seven primes in the first fifteen numbers.

△ Can you find a pair of starting numbers which produce more primes in the first fifteen numbers of the series?

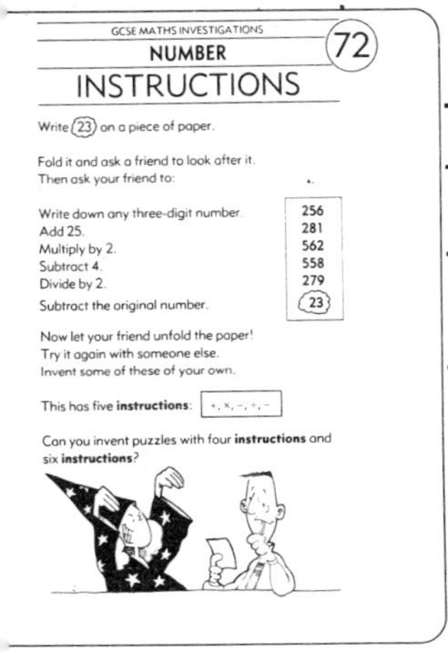
GCSE MATHS INVESTIGATIONS

NUMBER (72)

INSTRUCTIONS

Write (23) on a piece of paper.

Fold it and ask a friend to look after it.
Then ask your friend to:

Write down any three-digit number.	256
Add 25.	281
Multiply by 2.	562
Subtract 4.	558
Divide by 2.	279
Subtract the original number.	(23)

Now let your friend unfold the paper!
Try it again with someone else.
Invent some of these of your own.

This has five **instructions**: $+, \times, -, \div, -$

Can you invent puzzles with four **instructions** and six **instructions**?

GCSE MATHS INVESTIGATIONS

NUMBER

INSTRUCTIONS

72

△ Let the number be a:

add 25	$a + 25$
multiply by 2	$2a + 50$
subtract 4	$2a + 46$
divide by 2	$a + 23$
subtract original number	23

This has five instructions: $+, \times, -, \div, -$ in that order.

△ Here is a six-instruction puzzle:

add 10	$a + 10$
multiply by 20	$20a + 200$
divide by 4	$5a + 50$
subtract 40	$5a + 10$
divide by 5	$a + 2$
subtract original number	2

△ The order here is: $+, \times, \div, -, \div, -$

△ Four instructions:

double it	$2a$
add 10	$2a + 10$
halve it	$a + 5$
subtract original number	5

$\times, +, \div, -$

△ Investigate four instruction puzzles with different orders of operations. Is it possible to use $\times, +, \times, -,$ for instance?

△ Suppose you write down two numbers: a, b

add them together	$a + b$
double	$2a + 2b$
add 20	$2a + 2b + 20$

Investigate ways of finishing this off.

△ Introduce other operations, e.g. squares and square roots.

SHAPE

	APPARATUS	ACTIVITY
73 Trominoes	Squared paper Card	Arranging trominoes into grids
74 Overlaps	Tracing paper	Making shapes by overlapping polygons
75 Fiver	Card Scissors	Five-piece square dissections
76 Right angles		Drawing polygons containing right-angles
77 Square points	Dotty paper	Drawing squares
78 Diagonals		Diagonal properties of polygons
79 Symmetry	Dotty paper	Drawing symmetrical shapes
80 Tracer	Squared paper	Tracing squares on different grids

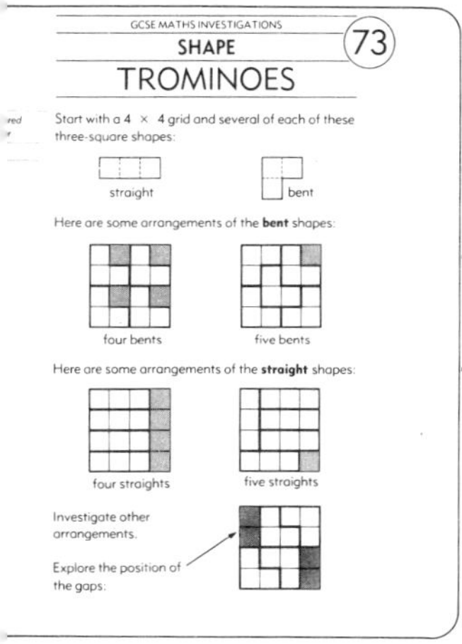
GCSE MATHS INVESTIGATIONS

SHAPE 73

TROMINOES

Start with a 4 × 4 grid and several of each of these three-square shapes:

straight bent

Here are some arrangements of the **bent** shapes:

four bents five bents

Here are some arrangements of the **straight** shapes:

four straights five straights

Investigate other arrangements.

Explore the position of the gaps.

GCSE MATHS INVESTIGATIONS

SHAPE

TROMINOES

73

Squared paper

Card

△ Some bent solutions:

four bents

Each of these solutions are based on these two gaps:

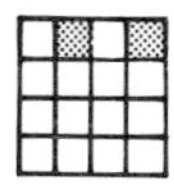

five bents

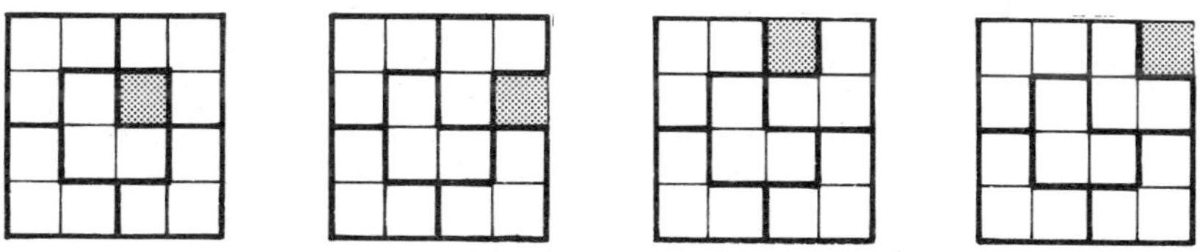

△ Some straight solutions:

four straights

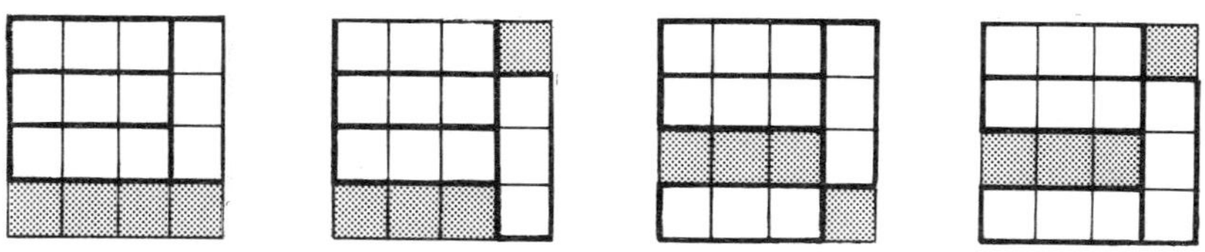

△ Extend to four-square shapes.

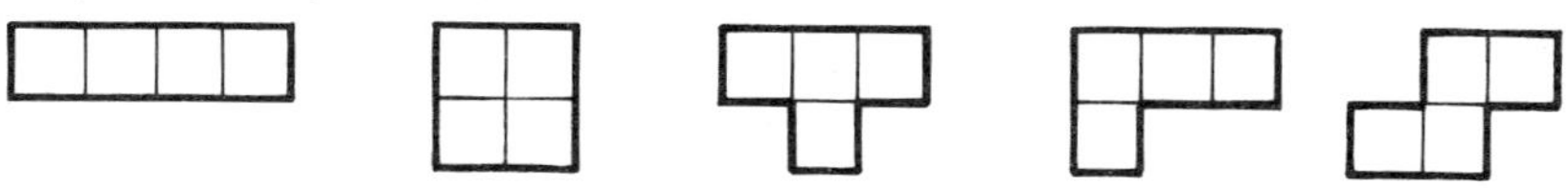

△ Change the size of the grid, e.g. rectangular grids.

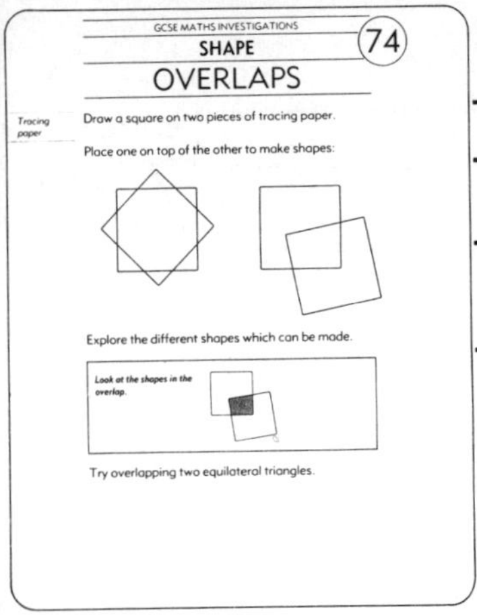
GCSE MATHS INVESTIGATIONS
SHAPE
74
OVERLAPS

Tracing paper

Draw a square on two pieces of tracing paper.

Place one on top of the other to make shapes:

Explore the different shapes which can be made.

Look at the shapes in the overlap.

Try overlapping two equilateral triangles.

GCSE MATHS INVESTIGATIONS

SHAPE

OVERLAPS

74

Tracing paper

△ Consider the shapes produced at the intersection:

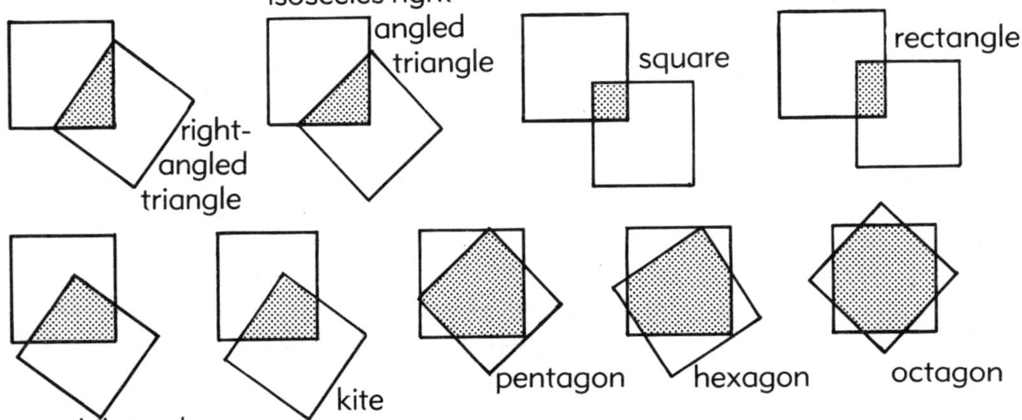

△ Consider overlaps which produce symmetrical shapes:

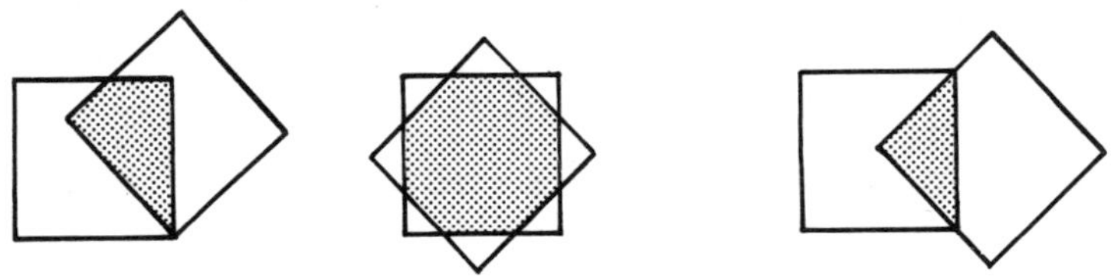

△ A different approach is to consider overlaps which create triangles:

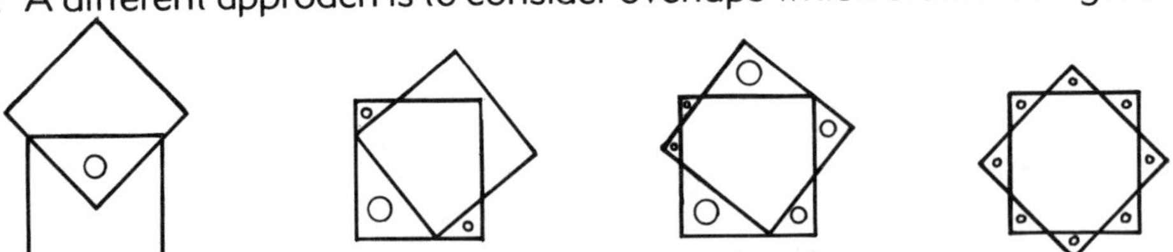

△ Try overlapping two equilateral triangles:

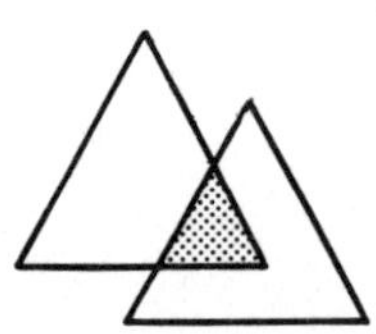

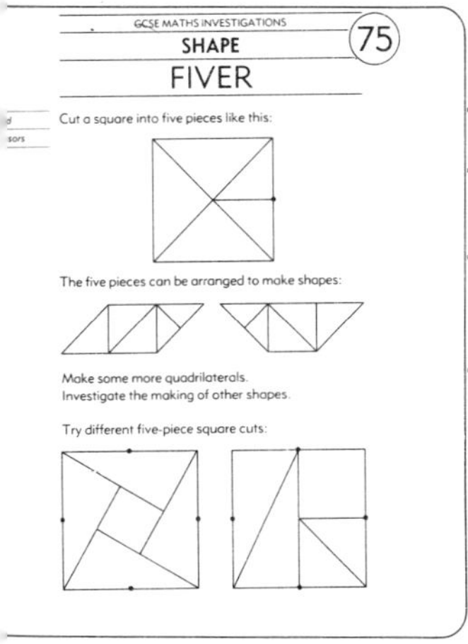
GCSE MATHS INVESTIGATIONS

SHAPE

FIVER

75

Cut a square into five pieces like this:

The five pieces can be arranged to make shapes:

Make some more quadrilaterals.
Investigate the making of other shapes.

Try different five-piece square cuts:

GCSE MATHS INVESTIGATIONS
SHAPE
FIVER
75

Card
Scissors

△ Many lines of investigation are possible:

△ Quadrilaterals:

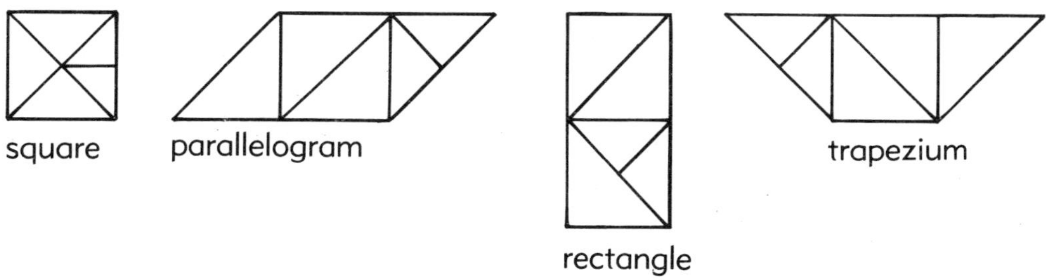

△ Symmetrical shapes

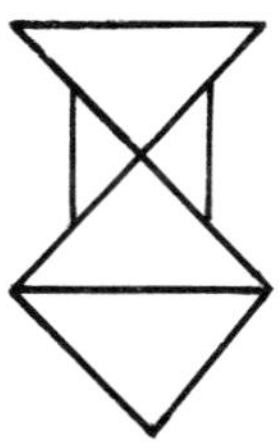

△ Polygons

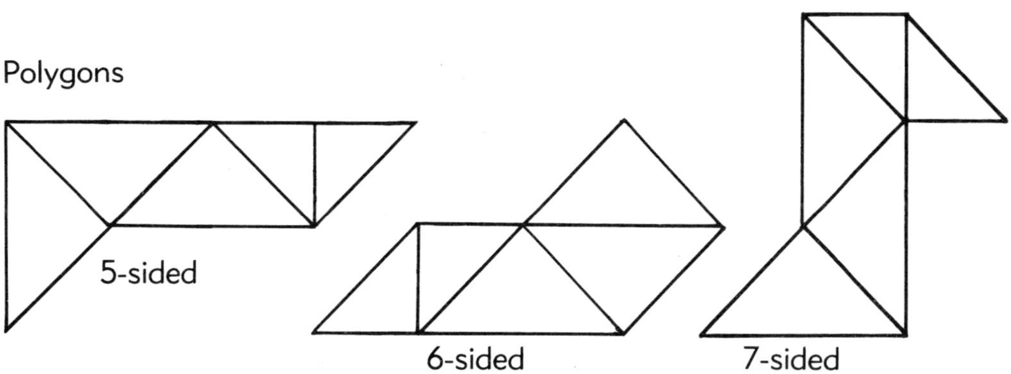

△ What will be the maximum number of sides?

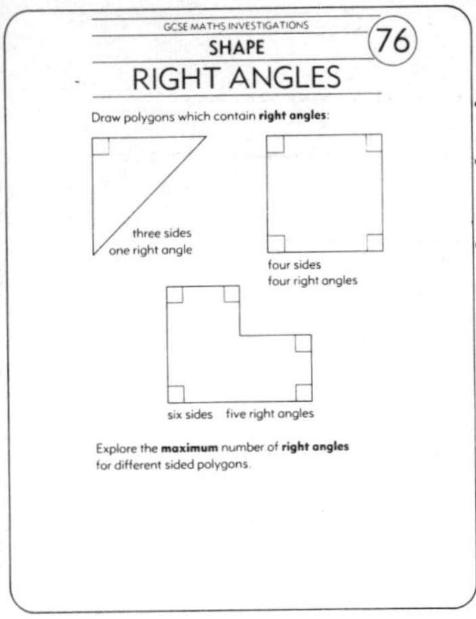

GCSE MATHS INVESTIGATIONS

SHAPE

76

RIGHT ANGLES

Draw polygons which contain **right angles**:

three sides
one right angle

four sides
four right angles

six sides five right angles

Explore the **maximum** number of **right angles** for different sided polygons.

GCSE MATHS INVESTIGATIONS

SHAPE

RIGHT ANGLES

76

△ Consider the maximum number of right angles for various polygons:

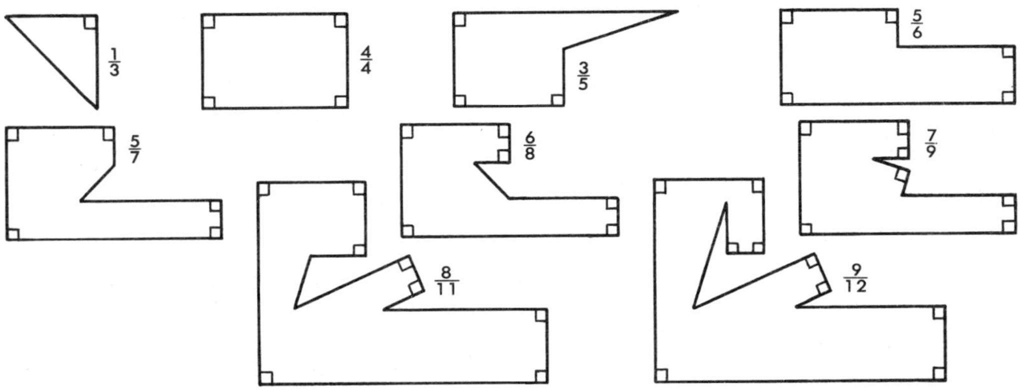

Let n be: the number of sides of the polygon:
if $n \leqslant 10$

***n*-odd**

Number of sides	Maximum number of right angles
3	1
5	3
7	5
9	7
⋮	⋮
n	$n - 2$

***n*-even**

Number of sides	Maximum number of right angles
4	4
6	5
8	6
10	7
⋮	⋮
n	$\frac{n}{2} + 2$

if $n > 10$

Number of sides	Maximum number of right angles
9 + 2	8 + 0
9 + 3]	8 + 1
9 + 4]	
9 + 5]	8 + 2
9 + 6]	
⋮	⋮

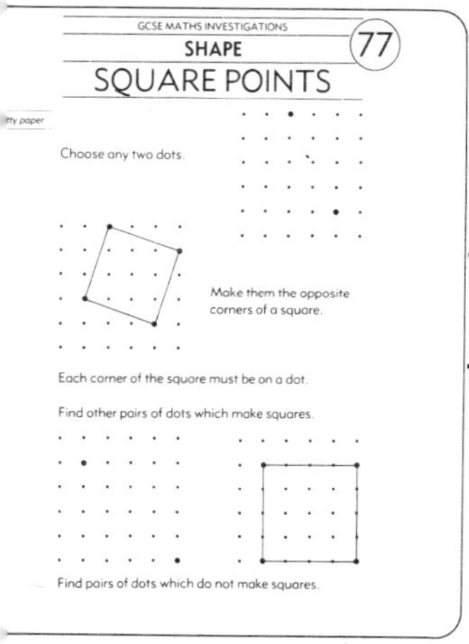
GCSE MATHS INVESTIGATIONS
SHAPE
SQUARE POINTS
77

Choose any two dots.

Make them the opposite corners of a square.

Each corner of the square must be on a dot.

Find other pairs of dots which make squares.

Find pairs of dots which do not make squares.

GCSE MATHS INVESTIGATIONS

SHAPE

SQUARE POINTS

77

Dotty paper

△ One approach is to choose a fixed point, X, and explore the squares which can be drawn from this point. Possible opposite corners to X are shown:

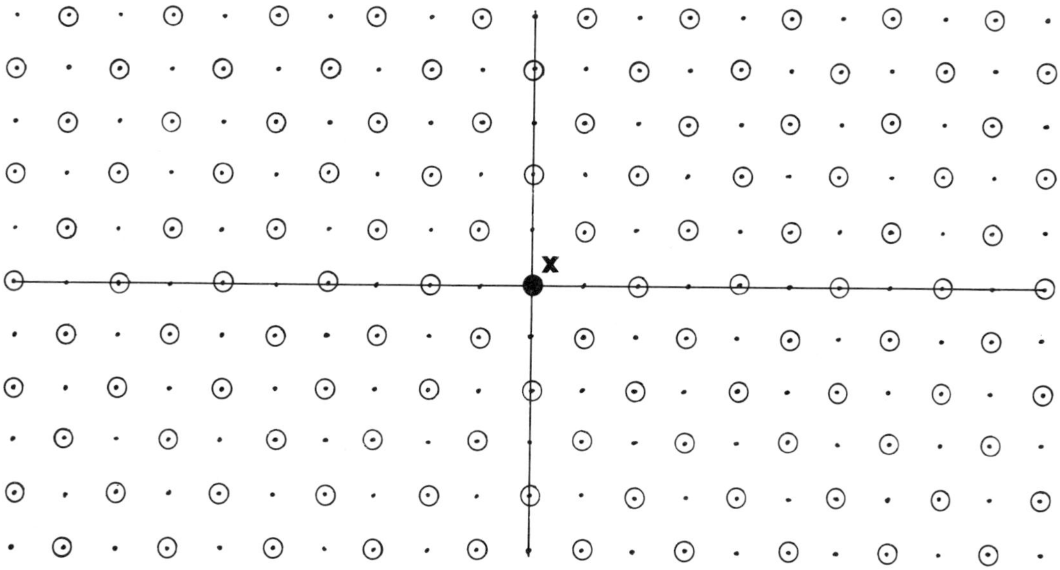

△ Let the fixed point have co-ordinates (0, 0).
Possible points which are the opposite corners of a square are:

(1, 1), (1, 3), (1, 5), (1, 7) ....
(2, 2), (2, 4), (2, 6), (2, 8) ....
(3, 1), (3, 3), (3, 5), (3, 7) ....
(those points whose co-ordinates are either both even or both odd).

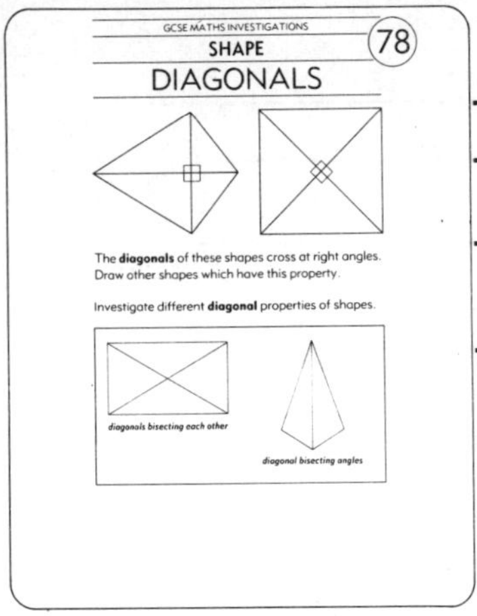
GCSE MATHS INVESTIGATIONS
SHAPE
78
DIAGONALS

The **diagonals** of these shapes cross at right angles.
Draw other shapes which have this property.

Investigate different **diagonal** properties of shapes.

GCSE MATHS INVESTIGATIONS

SHAPE

DIAGONALS

78

△ Quadrilaterals with diagonals crossing at right angles include:

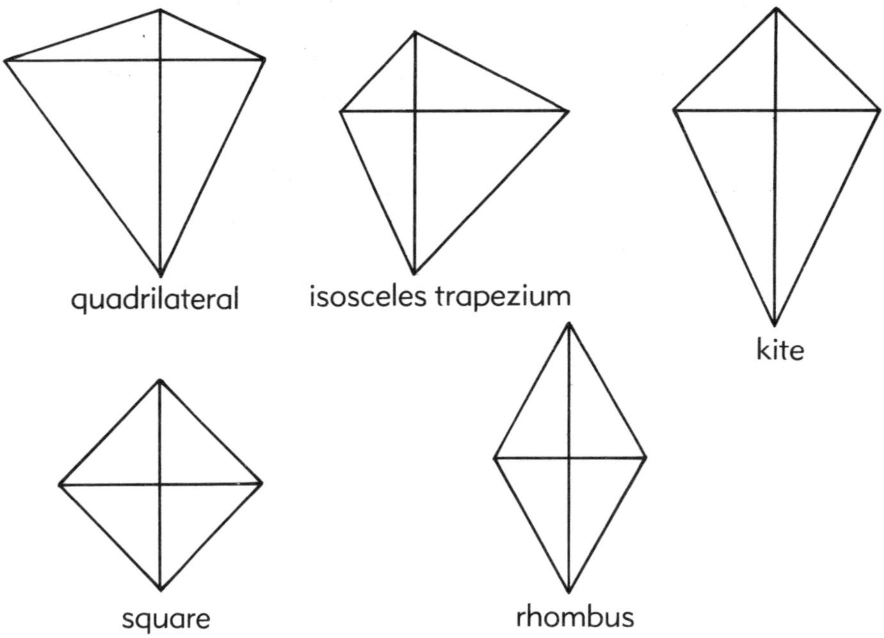

△ Other diagonal properties of quadrilaterals include:
one diagonal bisecting another
both diagonals bisecting angles

△ Investigate diagonal properties of regular polygons.

△ Which regular polygons can have diagonals crossing at right angles?

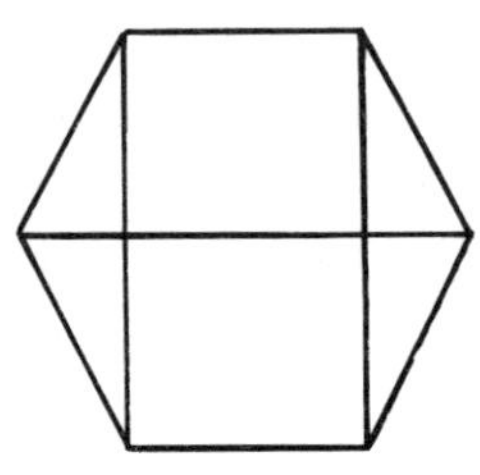

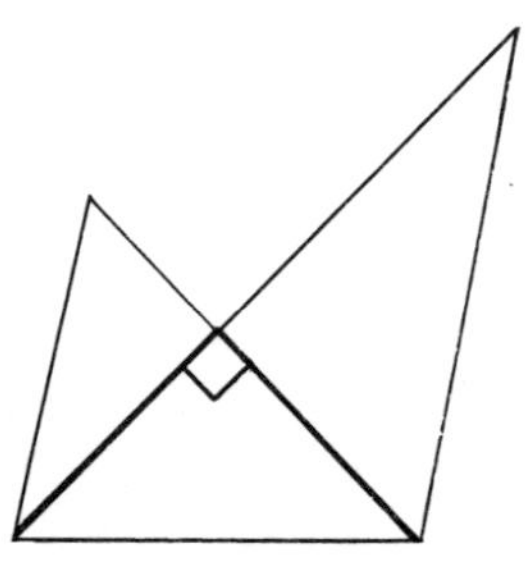

△ Consider concave polygons.

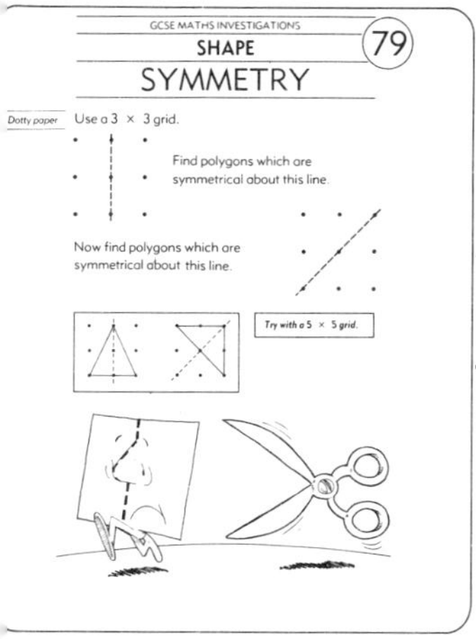

GCSE MATHS INVESTIGATIONS

SHAPE

SYMMETRY

79

Dotty paper

△ Some solutions include:

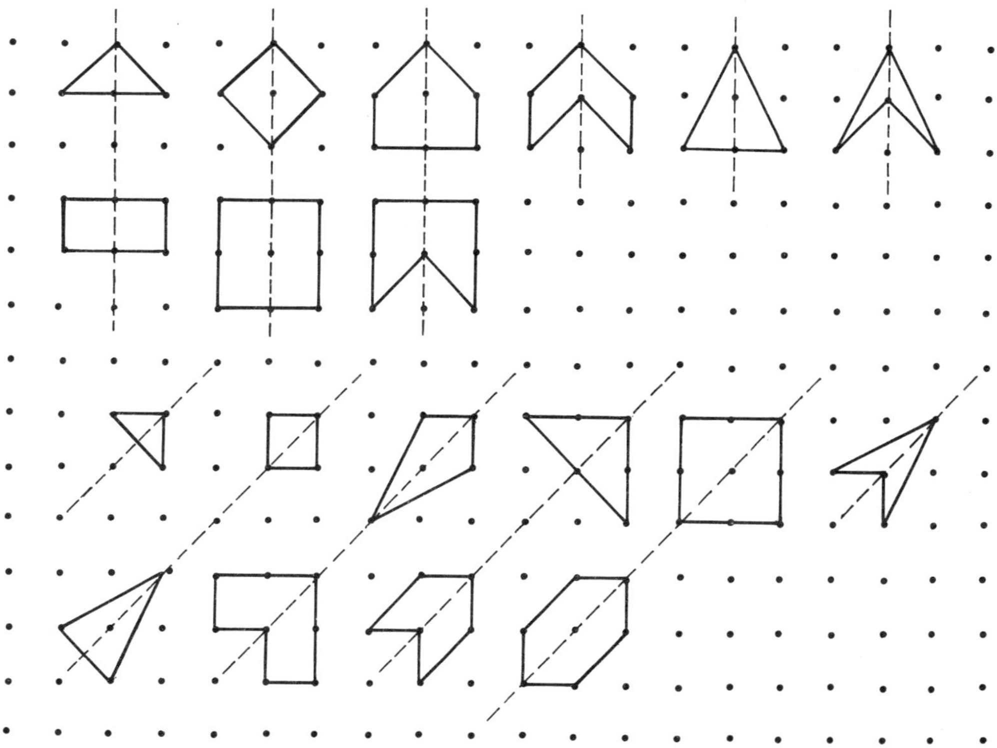

△ Which polygons have rotational symmetry about the centre dot? How many can be found?

△ Try 4 × 4 and 5 × 5 grids.

△ Look at symmetries on isometric dotty paper.

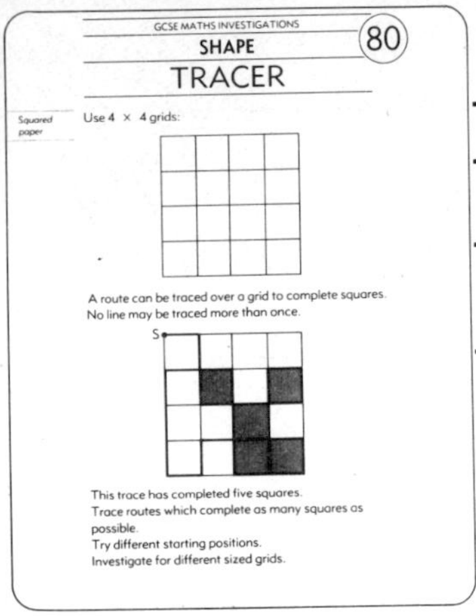
GCSE MATHS INVESTIGATIONS
SHAPE
80
TRACER

Squared paper

Use 4 × 4 grids:

A route can be traced over a grid to complete squares.
No line may be traced more than once.

This trace has completed five squares.
Trace routes which complete as many squares as possible.
Try different starting positions.
Investigate for different sized grids.

GCSE MATHS INVESTIGATIONS

SHAPE

80 TRACER

△ 4 × 4 grid:
Starting from a corner the maximum number of completed squares is ten.

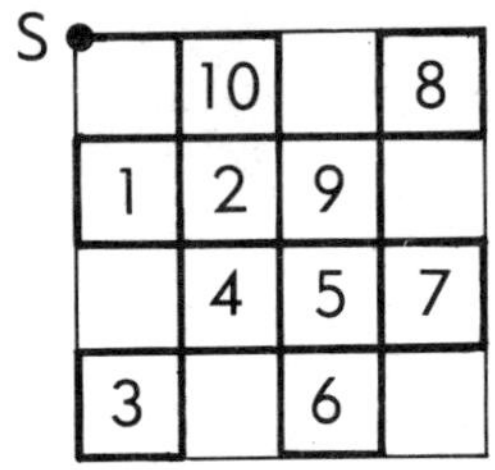

The order of completing the squares is shown.

△ How many ten-solutions can be found?
△ Try different starting positions:

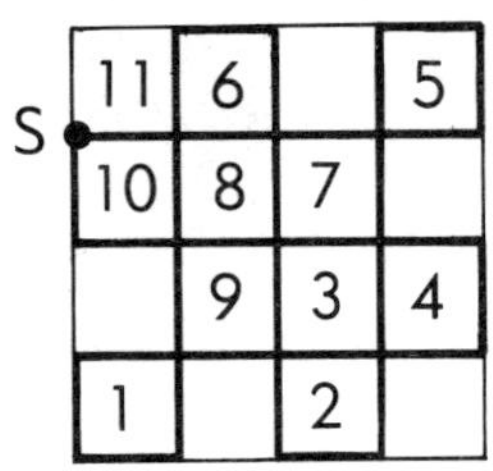

The maximum from this starting point is 11.

△ Maximum squares possible can be tabulated:

grid size	can be drawn	cannot be drawn
2 × 2	3	1
3 × 3	6	3
4 × 4	11	5
5 × 5	18	7
$n \times n$	$n^2 - 2n + 3$	$2n - 3$

△ Consider isometric grids.